A Reader's Guide to

GRAHAM
GREENE

A Reader's Guide to

GRAHAM GREENE

Paul O'Prey

THAMES AND HUDSON

For My Parents

First published in the United States in 1988 by
Thames and Hudson Inc., 500 Fifth Avenue,
New York, New York 10110

Library of Congress Catalog Card Number 88–50134

Typeset by Q-Set, Hucclecote, Gloucester
Printed and bound in Great Britain

Contents

> 'All things merge in one another –
> good into evil, generosity into
> justice, religion into politics . . .'

THOMAS HARDY

ABBREVIATIONS

ASOL   *A Sort of Life* (The Bodley Head, London, and Simon and Schuster, New York, 1971)

OM   *The Other Man: Conversations with Graham Greene* by Marie-Françoise Allain (The Bodley Head, London, and Simon and Schuster, New York, 1983)

WE   *Ways of Escape* (The Bodley Head, London, 1980; Simon and Schuster, New York, 1981)

Introduction

I

In *The Other Man* (1981) Greene likens the novelist to a double agent, in the way he 'condemns and sustains his characters by turns'. Greene himself resembles a double agent in another sense also, for as a writer he serves two different sorts of reader who in contemporary English literature are in an almost permanent state of conflict. On the one hand Greene is a consistent best-seller, capturing the imagination of an enormously wide and varied popular audience throughout the world; while on the other he is considered by many critics to be the best and most serious novelist writing in Britain today. No other writer since Dickens has so successfully combined immense popularity with complexity and craftsmanship.

This is not to say that critical opinion of Greene is undivided. Among some academics, his very popularity is a source of suspicion, but the main charges brought against his novels are that they are 'obsessive' and 'narrowly Catholic'. As I hope to show in this survey, although these charges have some truth when brought against certain of Greene's early and middle novels – particularly those for which he is best known, such as *Brighton Rock* and *The Heart of the Matter* – they have unfairly influenced his reputation to the detriment of his mature work, which in its richness and depth is his crowning achievement.

To take first the accusation against Greene that his novels are 'obsessive' expressions of his own troubled psyche. It is claimed by a number of critics that Greene does not depict reality in his novels (despite a highly realistic technique) but projects a mythical 'Greeneland', a reality distorted by his own view of life. This criticism was expressed most forcefully by Richard Hoggart, in *Speaking to Each Other* (1970):

① do you think H.O.M depicts reality or myth?

In Greene's novels we do not 'explore experience', we meet Graham Greene. We enter continual reservations about what is being done to experience, but we find the novels up to a point arresting because they are forceful, melodramatic presentations of an obsessed and imaginative personality.

Hoggart finds Greene's style forced, his structure and characters excessively controlled, his vivid backgrounds distorted, so that what emerges in the novels is a blend of rhetoric and caricature. This is to an extent indeed the case with certain of the early thrillers, such as *The Man Within, Stamboul Train, It's a Battlefield, A Gun for Sale* and *Brighton Rock*. In these, the author is clearly in absolute control of character and structure to the point that they seem manufactured and manipulated for the projection of a powerful personality and moral point of view. There were, of course, real gangsters on the racecourse at Brighton in 1938, some of them no doubt as brutal and evil as Pinkie. But Pinkie has too much of the legendary about him to be believed in as someone who actually walked and breathed outside the pages of the book. In the later novels, however, Greene achieves a greater range and depth, a greater subtlety and roundness, as characters speak for themselves rather than for their author, and even the most extreme settings, such as Papa Doc's Haiti or the *barrio* of the poor in Corrientes, have a strong sense of reality, reminding us that Greene is an accomplished journalist as well as a novelist.

As for the charge that Greene is a narrowly 'Catholic novelist', this ignores the broader humanism which is the real centre of his work, and which again is to be found mainly in his later novels. From *The Comedians* (1966) on, the religion of Greene's characters is far from being exclusive, for it is 'inextricably involved' in the political struggle for social justice and freedom. Even in the early novels, however, the religious element is wholly undogmatic and a long way from any orthodoxy, Catholic or otherwise. Indeed, Greene has frequently incurred the public disapproval of the Catholic Church for what he has written.

In *Why Do I Write?* (1948) Greene stated that as a novelist he was writing fiction, not propaganda, and defended his right to be 'disloyal' to the Church. As an artist, he wrote, he must be allowed to write 'from the point of view of the black square as well as from the white'. Thus many of his most sympathetically drawn characters are those in a state of doubt or even of unbelief. The driving force of faith seems to be for Greene, as it was for Miguel de Unamuno (see page 147), uncertainty. He is therefore particularly attracted to characters who inhabit a spiritual border-land, and who embody some form of paradox, such as 'holy atheists', 'Catholic agnostics', and sinful saints. Such paradoxes are part of the loyalty and betrayal themes central to ,Greene's work. In *The Other Man* he declared that the 'narrow boundary' between loyalty and betrayal is 'the paradox one carries within oneself'; it is 'what men are made of'. He reaffirmed too what he had written several years earlier in *A Sort of Life*, that if he were to choose a single epigraph for all his novels it would be taken from Browning's *Bishop Blougram's Apology*:

> Our interest's on the dangerous edge of things.
> The honest thief, the tender murderer,
> The superstitious atheist, demireps
> That love and save their souls in new French books –
> We watch these in equilibrium keep
> The giddy line midway.

Orthodoxy is questioned at every step in Greene's fiction. The two of his characters who come closest to a form of saintliness – the whisky priest in *The Power and the Glory* and Sarah in *The End of the Affair* – come to God through 'what the Church considers sin'. And the opposite of what the Church considers sin in the novels is not what the Church considers virtue, but love. Thus, despite all his sins, the whisky priest approaches a state of holiness through love, and François Mauriac, in *Men I Hold Great* (1951), considers the novel to be 'a great lesson . . . that, in the last day, according to the word of St John of the Cross, it is on love that [we] will be judged'.

Similarly, Greene continually casts doubt on the Church's authority in eschatological, as well as moral, matters. Even in the first of his so-called Catholic novels, *Brighton Rock*, a priest admits the inability of himself or any man to speak on God's behalf, when he tells Rose: 'You can't conceive, my child, nor can I or anyone the . . . appalling . . . strangeness of the mercy of God.'

Repeatedly, Greene creates situations in his fiction which test the teachings of the Church – extreme situations which show that for an omnipotent God each individual must by definition be a 'special case', to whom no man-made rule can apply. Thus when Scobie kills himself in *The Heart of the Matter* he is committing the sin of despair, the only sin, according to the Church, which God refuses to forgive; but again it is a priest who denies the Church's authority to judge the matter:

'For goodness' sake, Mrs Scobie, don't imagine you – or I – know a thing about God's mercy.'
'The Church says . . .'
'I know the Church says. The Church knows all the rules. But it doesn't know what goes on in a single human heart.'

Without anticipating here a discussion which properly belongs later in the treatment of individual novels, it is perhaps useful to give a brief account of Greene's own religious beliefs, as he has described them in interviews and in his autobiographical writings. In *The Lawless Roads* (1939), his account of religious persecution in Mexico following the socialist revolution there, Greene recounts a religious experience he had at the age of thirteen:

And so faith came to me – shapelessly, without dogma, a presence above a croquet lawn, something associated with violence, cruelty, evil across the way. I began to believe in heaven because I believed in hell, but for a long while it was only hell I could picture with a certain intimacy . . .

There then follows an elliptic account of his later conversion to Roman Catholicism: '. . . the Anglican Church could not supply the same intimate symbols for heaven' as life itself provided for hell, until 'slowly, painfully, reluctantly' he began to 'populate heaven'. The 'Mother of God' took the place of 'the brass eagle', and the example of the Curé d'Ars and Charles Péguy 'challenging God in the cause of the damned', gave him 'a dim conception of the appalling mysteries of love moving through a ravaged world'.
From this account, it would appear that Greene's conversion was based largely on an emotional response to Catholicism, and one suspects that aligning himself with a Church whose British members have traditionally been outsiders, as well as victims of

② Do you think its fair to judge Scobie solely on what the Church thinks is the ultimate unforgivable sin ?

persecution, may also have had an emotional appeal for him. But later, in *Ways of Escape* (1980), he maintained that he had not at the time been 'emotionally moved', only 'intellectually convinced', by the arguments for the existence of God put to him by a Catholic priest. Only after his visit to Mexico, where he had witnessed the way people were suffering for their faith, did he discover 'some emotional belief'.

It was in Mexico too that Greene's faith first gained a political dimension. For him, the religious persecution that followed the revolution there, combined with the outbreak of the Civil War in Spain, 'inextricably involved religion in contemporary life' – or, in other words, in politics. Religion and politics are mixed for the first time in *The Power and the Glory*, which is the story of an outlawed Mexican priest pursued by a fanatical socialist police lieutenant. But in the later novels, religion and politics become inseparable parts of the same theme. From *The Comedians* on, religious belief is seen inevitably to involve a political commitment to social justice on the part of the believer, for if he is commanded by Christ to love and side with the poor and oppressed, then he cannot stand aside, or wash his hands of responsibility like Pilate.

Greene's own political sympathies are with the Left, though despite a 'strong pull towards the Communist Party' he has consistently avoided membership of any particular group (his brief membership of the Communist Party at Oxford in the 1920s was, he claims, little more than a student joke). He has nevertheless been actively committed to fighting injustice and oppression in various parts of the world. Even now, in his eighties, he is 'involved', as is made clear by his later non-fiction works – *J'Accuse* (1982), an exposé of the Nice underworld, and *Getting to Know the General* (1985), an account of his friendship with President Genera Torrijos of Panama – as well as by his public support of the Sandinistas in Nicaragua, and the freedom fighters in El Salvador.

Because of his strong political commitments, Liberation Theology is the branch of the Church in which Greene would appear to be most at home, and Latin America, where Liberation Theology originated in the 1960s, offers him an ideal setting for the debate between Catholic and Communist which dominates

his later work. In *The Lawless Roads* Greene had written that
Catholicism 'had to rediscover the technique of revolution', and
in his later books it is seen to be doing just that. At the end of
The Comedians a Haitian priest delivers a liberationist sermon in
which he insists that Christians must be prepared to take part in
the political struggle against oppression even if it involves them
in acts of violence, for the Church condemns indifference more
than it condemns violence. This ethical problem is explored in
greater depth in *The Honorary Consul* (1973), in which a
Paraguayan priest, Father Rivas, actively takes up arms at the
risk of excommunicating himself and is even prepared to commit
the mortal sin of murder in the fight for liberation.

Greene finally reconciles his own personal religious and political beliefs in *Monsignor Quixote* (1982). In this, a priest whose
faith is based on doubt and a local politician whose belief in
Communism is wavering find common ground in uncertainty, in
human love and understanding, and in a shared opposition to
injustice and oppression. It is entirely in keeping with the nature
of that book and of Greene's personal commitments, that he
distributed the royalties it earned in Spain equally between the
Trappist monastery at Osera and the guerrillas in El Salvador.

Although Greene is, or has been, a Catholic (he now calls
himself a 'Catholic agnostic'), his reputation as a narrowly
Catholic writer of sectarian fiction must change as the range and
depth of his later work is fully appreciated. Greene writes as a
moralist as well as a realist, concerned with the moral complexity
and ambiguity at the centre of life as well as with the actual
experience of life, and his greatest achievement is in those books,
such as *The Power and the Glory* and *The Honorary Consul*, in
which he achieves a careful balance of the two, and in which he
combines the game of literature (with all the irony, humour,
excitement and commitment to plot of a truly popular novelist) with
a sensitive and profound treatment of important moral issues.

II

Greene has stated on several occasions his belief that one's
personality is determined in the first sixteen years of life, that 'in

the lost boyhood of Judas Christ was betrayed'. His own early life, as a member of a large, provincial, middle-class family at the beginning of the century, was 'extremely peaceful'. Reliving it in his autobiography, *A Sort of Life* (1971), he describes the 'happy atmosphere' of his home, despite the sense of distance he felt from his parents: his mother was 'remote' and 'indifferent' to the affairs of her young children, but they were 'devoted to each other from a distance'; his father, too, although extremely 'busy', was always caring. This childhood innocence was replaced by the 'horror' of experience when, at the age of thirteen, he became a boarder at Berkhamsted School, of which his father was then headmaster. The spartan and hostile environment of school, with its noisy, smelly dormitories, shared lavatories, and total lack of privacy, was a profoundly unpleasant experience for the sensitive child. This form of unhappiness is of course the common experience of many public schoolboys, but Greene's situation was aggravated by the peculiarity of his being the headmaster's son and having his home attached to the school – a happy home to which he was forbidden to retreat in his misery. The school was entered from home through a green baize door in his father's study. This door became a symbol for Greene of the border between innocence and experience, and he uses it in several short stories as well as in *The Ministry of Fear*, where it divides the 'arcadian' clinic and the 'hell' of the sick bay:

Ahead of him was the green baize door he had never seen opened, and beyond that door lay the sick bay. He was back in his own childhood, breaking out of dormitory . . .

To cope with 'the horror' both as a schoolboy and in later life, Greene devised various 'ways of escape'. Travel, danger and friendship have all offered Greene a temporary haven, but above all it is fiction – first as a reader, then as a writer – which has allowed him to escape most effectively.

Several of Greene's characters in the novels and short stories assert the biographical importance of childhood reading. Henry Pulling, in *Travels with My Aunt*, thinks that 'one's life is more formed . . . by books than by human beings', and blames his inability to love on the absence of the right books in his father's study; Wilditch in 'Under the Garden' reflects on his childhood and decides that 'His lot had probably been decided . . . when George was reading him *The Romance of Australian Exploration.* If a child's experience does really form his future life, surely he had been formed, not by Javitt, but by Grey and Burke.' Although Greene's literary influences can be traced to Stevenson, Conrad, James, and back to the seventeenth-century dramatists, he has said in *The Other Man* that the books which 'really influenced' him as a child were 'cloak-and-dagger novels, novels of adventure, and I believe that in a way it's adventure novels I'm writing today'. He mentioned, in particular, books by Captain Gilson, Anthony Hope, Stanley Weyman, John Buchan and Rider Haggard as having had a strong influence; but according to his essay 'The Lost Childhood', the book that 'let the future in' for him 'once and for all' was Marjorie Bowen's *The Viper of Milan*, which he read at the age of fourteen and which more than anything instilled in him the passion to write: 'From that moment I began to write. All the other possible futures slid away: the potential civil servant, the don, the clerk had to look for other incarnations.'

The Viper of Milan attracted Greene because it portrayed human nature not as black and white, as in the more conventional children's adventure books, but as black and grey, 'and I looked around and saw it was so'. The sense of doom hanging over the success of Bowen's hero, Visconti (the name of one of Greene's own characters in *Travels with My Aunt*, whom he delights in describing as 'a viper') had parallels for the young Greene in what he saw as the inevitably doomed success of his fellow pupils:

. . . the champion runner who would one day sag over the tape; the head of the school who would atone, poor devil, during forty undistinguished years; the scholar . . . and when success began to touch oneself too, however mildly, one could only pray that failure would not be held off for too long.

Reading 'The Lost Childhood', the reader can begin to understand how a child of Greene's background – a settled, conventional world of professional success – should as an adult and a writer be overridingly concerned with themes of failure, corruption, evil and betrayal:

It was no good in that real world to dream that one would ever be a Sir Henry Curtis, but della Scala who at least turned from an honesty that never paid and betrayed his friends and died dishonoured and a failure even at treachery – it was easier for a child to escape behind his mask. As for Visconti, with his beauty, his patience, and his genius for evil, I had watched him pass by many a time in his black Sunday suit smelling of mothballs . . .

This passage reveals how the sensitive and romantic child could find in the realms of imagination and fiction not only an escape from the daily horror of school life, with the nightmare of having to choose between betrayal of one's family or one's friends, but also a way of colouring and explaining this life and, perhaps more than anything else, a way of coping with it. In another essay, 'The Young Dickens', Greene wrote that the creative writer 'perceives his world once and for all in childhood and adolescence'; Green perceived his world once and for all when he entered the strange savage country through the green baize door of his father's study, with *The Viper of Milan* as his guide. But he also perceived his way through this country in 'that moment' when he began to write, when 'all the other possible futures slid away', and he discovered that for him the greatest 'way of escape' lay in the act of writing itself.

1 The Early Novels

Greene's first published novel was *The Man Within*, an historical adventure about smugglers on the Sussex coast in the nineteenth century, which had an initial success with readers and critics that Greene himself now finds 'inexplicable'. Although it is a remarkable technical achievement for a writer still in his early twenties, the book's style is derivative and sentimental, and all attempts at creating a sense of action and excitement are spoiled by the ambitious young author's unsuccessful pretensions to high moral seriousness and depth psychology.

The plot is extremely complex and often confusing. Andrews, the hero, is a young, sensitive romantic with a 'divided personality'. One side of him is a selfish coward, the other a stern moral critic (the 'man within' of the title). The book begins with the death of his tyrannical, bullying father, who had been the leader of a band of smugglers. Andrews is then persuaded to join the band by their new leader, Carlyon, who becomes both a friend and a father-figure to him. The smugglers had revered the father for his great courage and strength, and by comparison they find Andrews cowardly and weak. They continually criticize him for not being the man his father was, and in revenge Andrews betrays them to the revenue officers. The entire crew is arrested, except for Carlyon and two others, Harry and Joe. These three set off in pursuit of the traitor, who takes refuge in an isolated cottage. There he finds a beautiful young woman, Elizabeth, alone with her dead guardian, and falls in love with her.

Elizabeth persuades him to see through to the end what he has begun, and to prove to himself and the smugglers that he is as brave as any of them, by giving evidence at their trial in Lewes. However, when he reaches Lewes his resolve weakens and he decides against appearing in court. Then Lucy, the mistress of Sir Henry Merriman, the prosecution counsel, offers him her favours in return for evidence which will allow Sir Henry to secure a conviction. This episode contains the germ of moral ambiguity and complexity which was later to become Greene's speciality. Andrews finally finds the courage to appear in court out of lust for Lucy, and thus

. . . he was doing for a wrong reason what he had refused to do for a right. He had turned a deaf ear to what his heart, supported by the critic within, had asked of him, but he had capitulated at the first hungry wail his dirty, lusting body had uttered.

Lucy, on the other hand, strikes the bargain in order to *help* Merriman, whose heart is set on winning the case. Therefore, although she is betraying her lover (or 'keeper', as he cynically calls himself) by sleeping with Andrews, her betrayal is in fact evidence of a genuine feeling for him.

After giving evidence in court and claiming his 'reward' from Lucy, Andrews returns to the cottage where he and Elizabeth declare their love for each other and plan a future together. While he is out collecting wood, however, the three smugglers arrive at the cottage. Andrews runs for help but when he returns he finds Elizabeth dead, and Carlyon waiting for him. Carlyon explains that Joe had hurt her in an attempt to find out where Andrews was, but rather than give him away she had stabbed herself. There follows a hasty and unconvincing reconciliation between Andrews and Carlyon. Andrews decides to take the blame himself for what will obviously be seen by the authorities as murder, and sends Carlyon away. By doing this he not only atones for the betrayal of Carlyon but in a paradoxical way gains his long sought revenge on his father. Because he blames his father for all the weakness and cowardice in his own character, by an extension of doubtful logic he holds his father responsible for Elizabeth's death:

It was in any case, he felt dimly, not an act of the living which had crumbled life but of the dead, a victory for the old man who had preceded him in this cottage [Jennings, Elizabeth's dead guardian] and for his father. His father had made him a betrayer and his father had slain Elizabeth and his father was dead and out of reach.

As Andrews's thinking becomes increasingly confused, the weak side of his character is accused of 'murder' by the morally strong 'man within', and as the officers lead him away he sees the chance not only to take revenge on his father's spirit, but also to assert his true self once and for all:

> . . . Out of reach. But was he? His father's was not a roaming spirit. It had housed itself in the son he had created. I am my father, he thought, and I have killed her. At the thought the dry, strained despair in which he dwelt gave way before a kind of blessed grief.

At this moment the 'man within' finally takes control and reaches for the knife with which to stab himself.

The double suicide of Elizabeth and Andrews is an instance of the 'enormous brutality and despairing romanticism' which Greene says characterized his early attempts to write. It is particularly despairing in its implication that the only way man can break free from his determined fate is in the final escape of death, the only way he can take control of his life is by destroying it:

His father's had been a stubborn ghost, but it was laid at last, and he need no longer be torn in two between that spirit and the stern unresting critic which was wont to speak. I am that critic, he said with a sense of discovery and exhilaration.

The main failing of *The Man Within* is that the author is forcing the story to make general statements about life, themselves of a doubtful validity. He is trying to imbue the story with a greater significance than it is capable of holding, or he capable of expressing, and this use of force results in certain crudities of characterization. In particular, Elizabeth and Lucy, as the sexual extensions of the hero's divided personality, are mere lifeless embodiments of ideas, rather than 'real' people in whom we can believe.

The novel contains several of Greene's themes in embryonic form, such as loyalty and betrayal. The betrayal theme also has a number of religious overtones: Andrews betrays the one man in his life who loves him and who tries to help him, and a Biblical parallel is made by allusions to Carlyon as Christ and to Andrews as 'a sort of Judas'. On the whole, however, religion remains a vague element in the novel. God is 'indifferent', a shadowy, undefined force evident only in Elizabeth's life, though there are elements of the future Pinkie, the Catholic hero of *Brighton Rock*, in Andrews's bitter thoughts on God and the devil:

I would rather trust a devil to look after his own than a god . . . Thinking of the devil, he thought too of the stubbled face of Mr Jennings. Perhaps he would guard her, as she believed, through the crude force of jealousy. If love survived the body, as church people believed, why not also jealousy, spilt like a bitter wine into the unhoused spirit?

The Man Within exhibits an awkwardness when dealing with purity and sanctity, but a facility on the part of the young author for describing violence, hatred, lust and evil. Elizabeth's pure soul, for example, is literally too good to be true, but Andrews's alternating attraction to and repulsion from sexual contact, and his consuming sense of sin and guilt, are expressed with great effect. Such passages display what Vita Sackville-West, reviewing the book for the *Listener*, called 'a real sense of language', and stand out as having the genuine Greenian resonance:

He felt no fear of death, but a terror of life, of going on soiling himself and repenting and soiling himself again. There was, he felt, no escape. He had no will left.

II

Encouraged by the success of *The Man Within* and by an offer from his publishers of £600 a year for three years in return for three novels, Greene gave up his job as a sub-editor on *The Times* to become a professional novelist. Two more historical romances followed in quick succession: *The Name of Action*, published in 1930, and *Rumour at Nightfall*, published in 1931. Both books, however, were financial and artistic failures and Greene has consistently prevented their republication so that they can now be found only in libraries, or at collectors' prices in antiquarian bookshops.

The Name of Action is the story of Oliver Chant, an idealistic and wealthy young man who becomes involved in Ruritanian politics and in the overthrow of the dictator whose wife he has fallen in love with. Thus his political motives become confused with his personal motives, as was to be the fate of several later Greene heroes. In *Rumour at Nightfall*, Francis Chase, an English newspaper correspondent in search of a story in Spain, becomes involved with outlawed Carlist rebels, and again the hero's motives are made ambiguous by his love for a beautiful woman.

Both novels are turgid and unconvincing, the stories bogged down by the author's relentless analysis of his characters' thoughts and motives. In *Ways of Escape* Greene describes how at the time he was in danger of losing his way as a writer:

Both books are of a badness beyond the power of criticism properly to evoke – the prose flat and stilted and in the case of *Rumour at Nightfall* pretentious (the young writer had obviously been reading again and alas! admiring Conrad's worst novel, *The Arrow of Gold*), the characterization non-existent.

What is interesting, however, is that in these books Greene made his first attempt to introduce Catholicism into his fictional world. Both Chant and Chase are rational unbelievers who come into contact with Catholicism as yet another mysterious element of the exotic and romantic worlds into which they have strayed. They are at one and the same time attracted to and suspicious of its 'certainty', as the critic Richard Johnstone points out in *The Will to Believe*:

Both novels can be seen as statements of the problem facing the twentieth-century man attracted to religious commitment; they point both to the emotional need for faith, and to the impossibility of overcoming scepticism.

However, with the move to contemporary realism in his next book, *Stamboul Train*, Greene set aside the religious question to portray a secular world in almost wholly socio-political terms typical of the 1930s, and it was not until *Brighton Rock* in 1937 that he could confidently introduce religion into the foreground of one of his novels, or convincingly re-create the psychological processes of his adopted co-religionists.

The combined shock of a financial crisis *(Rumour at Nightfall* sold only 1,200 copies) and a particularly hostile review by Frank Swinnerton, opened Greene's eyes to the defects of what he had believed to be true art, and saved him from the disastrous attempt to be the new Conrad. He writes in *A Sort of Life*:

I knew the truth when I read it. There was nothing for me to do but dismantle all that elaborate scaffolding built from an older writer's blueprint, write it off as apprentice work and start again at the beginning. Never again, I swore, would I read a novel of Conrad's – a vow I kept for more than a quarter of a century . . . I had to begin again naked, and perhaps it was for that reason I chose an adventure story, imagining it might be easier to write, a mistake difficult to understand, since I had learnt with *The Name of Action* how hard it was to make physical action simple and exciting.

Stamboul Train marks the beginning of an entirely new phase in Greene's fiction: his début as a writer of contemporary thrillers, the genre in which he was to achieve his best work over the following decade. It was, Greene later wrote, the first time in his life that he deliberately set out 'to write a book to please, one which with luck might be made into a film'. Train films were extremely popular with cinema audiences at the time. Von Sternberg's *Shanghai Express*, Michael Balcon's *Rome Express*, Hitchcock's *The Lady Vanishes* and the Russian *Turksib* all enjoyed a fashionable success, as did Greene's *Stamboul Train* (retitled *Orient Express*), despite its being the last of these and, in Greene's words, 'far and away the worst, though not so bad as a later television production by the BBC' (which caused outrage in 1962 because of its explicit sexuality). The film solved Greene's immediate financial problems and the book itself had a considerable success. Greene himself finds that it is the only one of his books he is unable to re-read, because it is too heavily laden with 'the anxieties of the time and the sense of failure'. For others, however, it is perhaps the first of his novels that is readable today.

The main function of the train journey in *Stamboul Train* is a structural one: the action follows the Orient Express as it leaves Ostend and crosses Europe on its way to Constantinople. Although the action spills out at various stops along the line, for the most

part it is confined to the closed setting of the train. The closed
setting was a technique favoured by Conrad, who in many of his
novels isolated his characters on board a ship in order to let them
interact without interference from the outside, with the actual
setting becoming in the novelist's hands a microcosm of the
world. Greene uses the technique for the same purpose here.
The journey provides an opportunity to bring together in an
accidental fashion a broad range of characters who in some way
illustrate the statements Greene is making about contemporary
society. Greene follows the lives of several of the train's passengers,
rather than concentrating on one or two principal figures, and so
it is that encountered on the journey are a number of his favourite
'repertory' characters: a waif-like young girl (Coral); a Communist
facing disillusion (Dr Czinner); an inadequate priest (Opie); a
second-rate novelist (Savory); a journalist with little regard for
the truth (Mabel Warren), and so on.

As characters join the train along its route numerous sub-plots
are introduced, but the main action centres on Dr Czinner, an
exiled Communist revolutionary who is returning to his native
Belgrade to lead an uprising. As a young doctor in Belgrade,
Czinner had become frustrated in his attempts to help 'his people',
the poor, because he was unable to cure their main ailment,
poverty: 'He could not recommend rest to the worn-out or pre-
scribe insulin to the diabetic, because they had not the money to
pay for either.'

Having once been brought to trial as a revolutionary, Czinner
had escaped and endured a wretched exile in Britain, working
as a schoolmaster in Great Birchington-on-sea. The planned
uprising gives him new hope and even when he discovers on the
train that things have not gone according to plan and that the
revolution has in fact already failed, he decides to press on and
stand trial with the other conspirators, for at least his trial will
bring publicity to the cause. The trial, however, proves to be a
secret and unconstitutional military affair and Czinner's 'defence'
is a humiliating failure. His audience of one, the peasant soldier
whom he hopes to convert from 'the wrong service to the right'
with a final burst of rhetoric, remains unaffected, staring with
'wide stupid unhappy eyes' at Czinner, who is reduced to 'a tub
orator, no more'.

More than any other of Greene's 'entertainments', *Stamboul Train* is a potboiler. It contains all the ingredients to whet the appetite of an ABC audience: murder, revolution, love, and the loss of a chorus girl's virtue, all taking place on the Orient Express which, with its suggestion of luxury, romance and mystery, occupied a unique place in the popular mythology of the day. This emphasis on excitement and action results in characters who are uncomplicated to such a degree that they become stereotypes. Coral and Myatt, for example, recognize each other as known types in a world of casual pick-ups at the stage door, while Peters and his wife are placed by Coral in an instant:

'Who do you think you are?' She knew the answer: shopkeepers on a spree, going out to Budapest on a Cook's tour, because it was a little farther than Ostend, because they could boast at home of being travellers, and show the bright labels of a cheap hotel on their suitcases.

Characters are so sharply delineated that they tend to be caricatures. There is a little too much theatricality, for example, in the character of Mabel Warren, the drunken, 'manly' lesbian journalist with a pathetic emotional dependence on another stock figure, the coldly beautiful and shallow Janet Pardoe. There are, however, moments in Mabel's role as a hack journalist when she does take on a life of her own: in her ruthless, heartless pursuit of Dr Czinner, and in her contempt for the pompous novelist Savory, whom she interviews with cunning nastiness.

A caricature also, though a more effective one, is the armed robber Grünlich. He is a more unusual example of what used to be called the 'criminal classes' than one expects in a sensational novel of this kind. He callously exploits the lonely maid Anna in his attempt to rob the safe of her employer, whom he shoots in cold blood, and he later escapes the soldiers at the expense of Coral and Dr Czinner. His complete lack of scruples, and his inordinate vanity and pride in the evil he perpetrates, make him a deeply menacing figure, though Greene's surprisingly comic treatment of him – whispering a Hail Mary on the icy roof, joking to the clergyman about being 'a good runner', brooding on the injustice of it all at the end when he realizes that to the police the old and pathetic Czinner is far more important than he himself is – serves to undermine this portrait of total amorality.

Events on the journey to Constantinople change the lives of almost all the characters, though most of them (Janet, Mabel, Savory, Grünlich and Myatt) are, despite the various upheavals in their lives, essentially the same people when they arrive in Constantinople as they were when they left Ostend. The only exceptions are Coral and Czinner, who in fact never make it to their intended destinations. They are both changed by their experiences.

Coral is the prototype for a number of waif-like characters in Greene's novels. She is thin and pale, physically immature but alluring in a slightly perverse way, of limited intelligence and education, and in need of protection. She appears, with variations, in a number of books: as Molly in *It's a Battlefield*, as Loo in *England Made Me*, Anne in *A Gun for Sale*, Rose in *Brighton Rock* and Helen in *The Heart of the Matter*. On the journey Coral falls in love for the first time. This love seems inspired mainly by a pathetic gratitude to Myatt for his kindness and generosity, and by his promise to rescue her from the exhausting meanness of her present life. She tires of being 'decent' and loses her virginity to Myatt, happy at the thought of the security which being the mistress of a wealthy businessman offers. It is then that the outside world of politics and violence invades her private dream of happiness and destroys her plans, a shattering experience which, however, reveals an inner strength and sense of compassion as, unlike Grünlich, she gives up her own chance for freedom in order to return and help the dying Dr Czinner.

The treatment of the Communist Dr Czinner is sympathetic, though it shows Greene to be even at this stage distrustful of any political plans for a 'future based on what we are' (see page 33). As death becomes a reality for Czinner, he begins to see his atheism as a great emptiness. He had previously condemned religion as a fiction used by the rich to keep the poor in their place, but now he tentatively tries to reconcile himself with the faith of his childhood and turns to the clergyman, Opie, for help. In a brief, amusing scene, Opie reveals not only an inherent lack of religion but also a lack of humanity, completely failing to understand Czinner's plea for help and instead deftly trying to turn from the topic of religion to the preferred subjects of cricket and his book. He discusses the latter with the same complacency as the novelist, Savory: '. . . I intend to strike deeper. The Roman books are, what shall I say, too exclusively religious.' Opie's similarity to Savory is also hinted at by Savory's unexpected entry, which rescues Opie from the embarrassment of Czinner's earnestness and his own nervous monologue on confession.

In Czinner's final moments, when he realizes he has 'no more duties to anyone but himself', his confused thoughts return again to his childhood faith. The 'Christian training' given him by his parents then takes 'an ironical revenge' as he begins to wonder 'in what he had erred and how it was that others had succeeded'. He has the sensation of falling, and the faces of his dead parents appear to tell him they are grateful, 'that he had done what he could, that he had been faithful'. At this point, different sorts of faith become confused as Czinner decides that he has been 'damned by his faithfulness' – faithfulness to political ideology. Then the narrative switches suddenly back to Coral's point of view. As if reading Czinner's thoughts, she thinks 'he had been too faithful' and decides, like him, that being faithful 'doesn't pay':

Her thoughts returned with stupid fidelity to Myatt . . . But she was aware all the time that there was no quality in Myatt to justify her fidelity; it was just that she was like that and he had been kind. She wondered for a moment whether Dr Czinner's case was not the same; he had been too faithful to people who could have been served better by cunning.

The implication is that secular beliefs and human attachments are no substitute for faith in God, but the treatment of this question in what is intended as a light, entertaining novel is naturally superficial.

The most obvious difference between *Stamboul Train* and the earlier novels is that it is set in the present, and this shift from historical romance to contemporary realism clearly called for an equivalent modernization of technique. The first three novels were, in Greene's own words, 'vague, shadowy, out of focus', their images blurred in an abundance of adjectives, similes and other attempts at 'fine writing'. *Stamboul Train* has a simple style which conveys a sense of action and excitement much more directly. The influence of Conrad was not dead – it was to reappear forcefully in the next novel, *It's a Battlefield*, perhaps because there Greene was attempting something more serious and ambitious – but a new influence can be detected in *Stamboul Train*: the cinema, itself a product and symbol of the modern world Greene was trying to portray. The reviewer in the *New York Times Book Review* noticed that the style of the novel 'smacked' of the cinema, but it was V. S. Pritchett, writing about *It's a Battlefield* in the *Christian Science Monitor*, who first recognized Greene's cinematic method as a 'technical innovation', and who predicted that Greene had initiated a movement which could 'wean' the English novel from its 'present competent dullness'.

Despite Greene's clear contempt for Savory, the successful novelist in *Stamboul Train*, he has him make a self-conscious reference to these experiments with the cinematic method, as he looks out of the carriage window and thinks about how to describe the passing scenery in words: 'One thing the films had taught the eye . . . the beauty of landscape in motion.' Greene captures the sense of the train's movement by 'pointing' his 'camera eye' through the window and allowing it to record the landscape as it flashes past. There are several examples of this, but the following passage is remarkable also for the characteristically startling image (the burning castles) with which Greene often captures the reader's attention and imagination, and also for the way in which the point of view shifts subtly from Myatt to the people waiting at the station. Thus the observed become the observers while the 'camera eye' technique is maintained:

The great blast furnaces of Liège rose along the line like ancient castles burning in a border raid. The train lurched and the points clanged. Steel girders rose on either side, and very far below an empty street ran diagonally into the dark, and a lamp shone on the café door. The rails opened out, and unattached engines converged on the express, hooting and belching steam. The signals flashed green across the sleepers, and the arch of the station roof rose above the carriage. Newsboys shouted, and a line of stiff sedate men in black broadcloth and women in black veils waited along the platform; without interest, like a crowd of decorous strangers at a funeral, they watched the line of first-class coaches pass them, Ostend – Cologne – Vienna – Belgrade – Istanbul – the slip coach for Athens.

The same 'camera eye' technique is used inside the train, to follow a character down the moving corridor or close in on a relevant conversation. Scenes are cut and juxtaposed in the manner of film editing, contrasting simultaneous conversations, shifting from the intimate interior of the first-class compartments to the public corridor, to the crowded third-class coaches and to the restaurant car. Here all the characters can be brought together, and the action 'cuts' rapidly from table to table:

'Look through there in the first class, Amy. Can't you see her? Too good for us, that's what she is.'
'With that Jew? Well, one knows what to think.'
'I have the greatest respect, of course, for the Roman Catholic Church,' said Mr Opie. 'I am not bigoted. As an example of organization . . .'
'So?'
'I am silly now.'
'Juicy.'
'No, no, that one's not juicy.'

Another feature of the highly visual style Greene is developing here is what K. W. Gransden in 'Graham Greene's Rhetoric' has called the 'catalogue', which consists of 'a series of concrete descriptive images, evoking a character or location – a kind of montage technique like that used in the cinema . . . and more especially the thriller movie . . .' Greene evokes the physical surface of the immediate environment with particular, concrete details which are selected because they embody what Gransden calls 'the essential features of a location or the moral landscape within which a character moves'. It is a technique that is used only partially in *Stamboul Train*:

. . . the drenched deck, the smell of steam and oil and Bass from the bar, the shuffle of black silk . . .
. . . the ewer and the basin on the liver-coloured washstand, the chipped gilt mirror, the iron bedstead, the chamber pot, the holy picture . . .

In later novels, however, Greene was to develop the catalogue to the extent that it has become an unmistakable characteristic of his style and one of the reasons why that style is so tempting to parodists.

III

Like many young middle-class intellectuals of the 1930s, Greene was drawn to the Left in politics. In *It's a Battlefield*, the most overtly political of his early novels, he paints a broad and graphic picture of injustice and inequality in contemporary society, displaying an awareness of, and deep concern for, the suffering endured by the millions of low paid and unemployed during the Depression. Jim Drover, a bus driver and a Communist, has hit and accidentally killed a policeman whom he thought was going to strike his wife, Milly, during a political demonstration in Hyde Park. Jim is subsequently found guilty of murder and sentenced to death. The novel, which is an account of his appeal for clemency, exposes the cynical processes of a justice system designed to protect vested interests. Jim's fate is seen ultimately to rest not on his innocence or guilt, but on public opinion, as manipulated by the press, and on the pragmatic concern of politicians for their own careers.

The novel's central characters are the Assistant Commissioner of Police, who has been asked by an unnamed Cabinet Minister to assess what public reaction would be to a reprieve, and Jim's brother, Conrad, who is fighting for the reprieve but who becomes deeply embittered and finally maddened by frustration at not being able to obtain it. As Conrad's reason slowly disintegrates, he decides to seek revenge against society by killing the Assistant Commissioner, who has become for him a symbol of the heartlessness and injustice of authority. He obtains a gun, tracks down the Assistant Commissioner and shoots him, only to find that the gun is loaded with blanks. At the same time, ironically, Jim Drover is reprieved. The irony is twofold, for not only is Conrad's revenge made unnecessary by the reprieve, but on being informed of the commutation of his sentence to life imprisonment Jim tries to commit suicide, for the prospect of a life spent in prison seems to him worse than death.

Conrad's walk through the streets in pursuit of the Assistant Commissioner, his mind deranged and his gun loaded with blanks, is an interesting variation on the thriller's usual melodramatic chase: the pursuer, the policeman, becomes the pursued, realizing it but not recognizing his pursuer nor understanding the danger he is in (which itself turns out to be illusory). The genuine excitement and the skill with which Greene follows the chase from both points of view, while revealing through interior monologue Conrad's steady mental disintegration, make it a superb climax to the story and, as Greene has rightly said, as successful as anything he has written since.

Although the Assistant Commissioner and Conrad are the central characters, they do not dominate the action. Since the appeal is considered from every angle (except, in the event ironically, Jim's own), Greene can present here, as in *Stamboul Train*, a broad range of characters. The feelings and considerations of Milly, Conrad, and Jim's fellow Communists, as well as those of the policemen, journalists and politicians with whom Jim's fate actually rests, are all explored. This allows Greene to paint a socially realistic portrait of the various classes and their respective environments. As we shall see, however, he also goes beyond the purely contemporary and the purely sociological to explore the relationship between social injustice and the fundamental weaknesses of human nature.

The novel opens in an exclusive West End restaurant which the Minister's private secretary has chosen for his meeting with the Assistant Commissioner. The private secretary represents power and money, and, like the other upper-class characters in the story (the dilettantish but socially aware Lady Caroline, and the wealthy Communist intellectual, Surrogate), his material possessions are emphasized to the extent that they become an integral part of his character:

His face was like the plate-glass window of an expensive shop. One could see, very clearly and to the best effect, a few selected objects: a silver casket, a volume of Voltaire exquisitely bound, a self-portrait by an advanced and fashionable Czechoslovakian.

The luxury and security of the private secretary's life is compared to the drab, poverty-stricken world of Conrad, Milly, and Milly's sister Kay, who works in a match factory. The match factory itself represents work in the novel, and is a heartless environment of drudgery, accident and ruthless exploitation:

A hand to the left, a hand to the right, the foot pressed down. A finger sliced off so cleanly at the knuckle that it might never have been, a foot crushed between opposed revolving wheels. 'It never hurt her . . .' Sickness benefit; half wages; incapacity; the management regrets.

The mechanistic nightmare of the factory girls is described somewhat expressionistically, organized as it is on exactly the same lines as the prison in which Jim is held:

'That's Block A. The new employees go there for the simplest processes. Then if they work well they move to Block B, and so to Block C. Everyone in Block C is a skilled employee. Any serious mistake and they are moved back to Block B.'

Comparisons such as this one between workers and prisoners are made throughout the novel as part of the fundamental comparison between rich and poor, seen here by Conrad mainly in terms of power and powerlessness:

'We ought to use influence. Everything goes by influence,' [Conrad] said, thinking of the brothers on the board, the nephew in the clerks' room. But he was daunted the next moment by his own and Milly's insignificance. He heard the world humming with the voices of generals and politicians, bishops and surgeons and schoolmasters . . .

The injustice Greene is attacking in *It's a Battlefield* is not just the injustice which can condemn an innocent man to death out of political expediency, but the wider injustice of a society in which wealth and power are so unevenly distributed. The strongest statement of this, the political and economic argument of the novel, comes from Lady Caroline, who asks the Assistant Commissioner:

'Do you believe in the way the country is organized? Do you believe that wages should run from thirty shillings a week to fifteen thousand a year, that a manual labourer should be paid less than a man who works with his brains?'

The Commissioner is aware of the unfairness of the system he upholds though he tries to detach himself from responsibility for it, and is the first of a number of Greene's characters to be likened to Pilate:

Justice is not my business; politics are not my business. God help the
men responsible for the way that life is organized; I am only a paid
servant, doing what I am told; I am no more responsible than a clerk is
responsible for the methods of the business he serves.

Greene contrasts this negation of responsibility with the almost
neurotic burden of responsibility assumed by the actual clerk,
Conrad. At school Conrad had been shown films of starving
children: '. . . [and] only Conrad knew; only Conrad felt the
unbearable responsibility for their starvation, could not forget
them . . .'

In the character of Conrad, Greene is anticipating what was to
become one of his major themes, the dangerous emotion of pity.
Conrad's sense of responsibility for others leads him to pity
them, as when he sleeps with Milly:

If he had felt the slightest lust, he would have fled; it was the unexcite-
ment in his love, the element of pity, that kept him there . . .

Conrad concludes that to love and care, as he loves and cares
for Jim and Milly, means inevitably to suffer, and that it is not
just organized society but human life itself which is fundamentally
unfair:

He became aware with sudden clarity how injustice did not belong only
to an old tired judge, to a policeman joking in Piccadilly [the Assistant
Commissioner]; it was as much a part of the body as age and inevitable
disease. There was no such thing as justice in the air we breathed, for it
was those who hated and envied and married for money or convenience
who were happy. Death could not hurt them, it could only hurt those
who loved . . .

In *Stamboul Train* life was seen in terms of a train journey, but
here it is seen as a battle fought in fog, an image derived from
A. W. Kinglake's description of the Battle of Inkerman which
Greene takes as his epigraph. This battlefield was 'made up of
nothing except small numberless circlets commensurate with
such ranges of vision as the mist might allow at each spot':

In such conditions, each separate gathering of English soldiery went on
fighting its own little battle in happy and advantageous ignorance of the

general state of the action; nay, even very often in ignorance of the fact that any great conflict was raging.

For Greene this was a fitting description of the individual's isolation and confusion in a bewildering urban environment. It is a world in which the avoidance of moral responsibility by individuals, each struggling with his own existence, is almost an inevitability, as the Assistant Commissioner is aware: 'The truth is, nobody cares about anything but his own troubles. Everybody's too busy fighting his own little battle to think of the, the next man.'

Some people on the battlefield, however, deliberately create their own fog so as not to see, so as to avoid facing up to a painful reality and to avoid any responsibility. This is the case with the pseudo-Communist journalist, Conder. He dramatizes his every action to the extent that he in fact leads a fictitious double life:

A man passed him in the corridor walking rapidly and called over his shoulder: 'Well, Conder, how are the Reds?' Conder nodded silently without a smile. Conder who was no longer the backbone of the country, but the hidden hand. Conder the revolutionary. But flick, flick, like the leaves of a book Conder's character turned and changed, and by the chief sub-editor's chair he was again the able journalist, the husband and the father.

The husband and father role is a total fantasy, for Conder has no wife or children and lives alone, but the only way he can cope with the misery of his actual existence is by pretending he lives another happier and more meaningful one. His political involvement is also a fantasy, while as a journalist no story leaves his hands 'without the truth unheightened'.

Surrogate, the wealthy Communist intellectual, is also incapable of facing reality and escapes into the 'lovely abstractions' of ideological generalizations. His involvement in politics is not a genuine commitment but the expression of an enormous egotism. His speech at the Party meeting in defence of Drover shows only a wilful blindness and an indulgence in romantic fantasy: 'He had no picture in his mind of the condemned cell, the mask, the walk to the shed; he saw Caesar fall and heard Brutus speak . . .'

Individuals like Drover continually intrude on and destroy Surrogate's fantasy, forcing reality on him:

> He resented even Drover's intrusion as an individual to be saved and not a sacrifice to be decked for the altar. In a cause was exhilaration, exaltation, a sense of Freedom; individuals gave pain by their brutality, their malice, their lack of understanding.

This need for a cause, or a belief, is something he shares with Jules, who runs the café above which Conder lives. Jules wants to escape 'the counter and the tea urn, the "weights" and the heartless flippancy of the café', and in a moment of irony he envies the Assistant Commissioner and his men:

> He would have dedicated himself to any cause, any individual, even a woman, if he could have been as serious as those six policemen driving down Charlotte Street.

The irony lies in the fact that the Assistant Commissioner also feels the lack of anything to believe in. He is a man who does his job not out of any high motive but solely out of a sense of duty to the organization that pays him:

> It was only when he was tired or depressed or felt his age that he dreamed of an organization which . . . would enlist his fidelity because of its inherent justice, its fair distribution of reward, its reasonableness.

Greene does not suggest here that any such 'organization' is possible. Although he is clearly sympathetic to the Communist point of view in the novel, Communism itself is unable to solve the problem because like any other form of secular commitment it is based on the capacity for good or evil in individual human beings. This is a theme he develops further in *The Power and the Glory*, though *It's a Battlefield* shows that his position is already clear – a position best summed up in a sentence from *Journey Without Maps*, the account of his walk through Liberia in 1935, a year after *It's a Battlefield* was published:

> There are others, of course, who prefer to look a stage ahead, for whom Intourist provides cheap tickets into a plausible future, but my journey represented a distrust of any future based on what we are.

A possible solution is, however, vaguely hinted at towards the end of the novel: the commitment to a cause greater than man himself. Thus Jules, who clings to the religious practices of his upbringing, finds that the need to devote himself to something or someone worthwhile is at least temporarily satisfied in church, surrounded by the 'hideous statues of an uncompromising faith': '. . . he was given confidence, an immense pride, a purpose. However lost in the café, forgetful of knives and sugar, here he was at home.'

The only other character to enjoy the solace of a religious faith is Lady Caroline, though the nature of that faith is vague ('not Christianity'). Like Jules she is strongly affected by the external manifestations of religion, possessing a curious, eclectic mixture of religious artefacts which suggests spiritual confusion: 'incense, Indian idols (there were several in the spare bedrooms), ikons (there was one on the staircase), pictures of the Virgin (they were everywhere) . . .'

At the end of the story the Assistant Commissioner – shocked by Conrad's attempted murder and Jim's attempted suicide, desperate actions which are the alarming symptoms of a sick society – envies Caroline her capacity for faith. However, he is also cynically aware of the opportunist and changeable nature of her belief:

If I had faith, he thought wryly; if I had any conviction that I was on the right side; Caroline has that; when she loses it, she has only to change her side.

Like many of Greene's novels, *It's a Battlefield* ends with the appearance of a priest. All possibility of human justice having been discredited, the author almost inevitably must come to the question of divine justice in a world in which the Creator, in the words of John Newman, seems to have 'discarded us from His presence'. Jim's attempted suicide causes the priest to resign from his job as prison chaplain. He tells the Assistant Commissioner: 'I can't stand human justice any longer. Its arbitrariness. Its incomprehensibility.' The Assistant Commissioner replies by asking if divine justice isn't 'much the same', but the question is left unanswered. The priest avoids a direct response by lamely pointing out that he has 'no complaint against His mercy' and that one can't hand in one's resignation to God (though that is surely what Jim Drover had been attempting to do).

The story of Drover's crime and his appeal against the death sentence is a real-life situation, very much like a piece of actual copy Greene might have been required to handle in the course of his work on *The Times*. Newspapers themselves are important in the novel and in fact it could be said that the novel is, to some extent, actually about the part newspapers play in society. The sensational and unrealistic treatment of events by the press, such as the meeting of the local Communist Party to discuss Drover's appeal ('Drama at Red Meeting – Clash Behind Locked Doors') is ironically juxtaposed with the dull human reality. But the true power of this myth-making media is recognized by Milly. Disillusioned in 'justice', she sees that Jim's fate is a question of politics and that the only way to influence politicians is through the right number of column inches. She makes this clear in her conversation with the journalist Conder: ' "I don't want justice," Milly said. "I've seen enough of it. I was in Court every day . . . I want publicity." '

The city streets are full of newspaper vendors and quotations from newspapers are numerous, as if individuals in this modern, mass society cannot escape the intrusion of the outside world into their own private one. Newspapers are also used in the novel to reinforce the illusion of reality. Thus authentic sounding headlines following the activities of the Prime Minister of the day ('Mr MacDonald Flies to Lossiemouth', 'Disarmament Conference Adjourns') are intermingled with equally plausible headlines following the fictional events inside the novel: ' "Home to Lossiemouth", "3.30 Results", "Insured?", "Appeal Fails", "Midday Runners". . .'

This use of newspapers helps to create a realistic portrait of contemporary life in the city, which itself is vividly evoked through the use of highly visual, concrete imagery. Again Greene's technique here 'smacks of the cinema'. A good deal of the novel comprises 'exteriors', scenes 'shot' in the streets. Characters travel by car, bus or foot, or simply wait, and while they are in the streets the author, using the 'camera eye' technique, observes and records. Like the cameraman or film editor, Greene is highly selective with his images: faces in the crowd, newspaper headlines, shop windows, are all chosen to create a certain effect, an impression of a landscape which tells us something about its inhabitants. The following scene, for example, in which the Assistant Commissioner and his subordinates rush through the West End traffic on their way to arrest a mad murderer, combines action with a description of a physically sordid and spiritually empty landscape. It ends, too, with a wonderfully ironic thought-association between the fairground rifle and the firearms used by the police and criminals, which points to an absurd element in society's violence:

The high squeal of the Wolseley's hooter pierced through a traffic block; cars ground their brakes, a policeman raised his hand, and they were shaken out into Charing Cross Road temporarily bare of traffic. The whores flowed down one pavement and up another; flat dago faces printed on song sheets filled the window of a music shop and a salesman inside played with passionate melancholy: 'My Baby Don't Care'. A row of men peered into peepshows, and 'A Night in Paris' and 'What the Butler Saw' and 'For Women Only' rattled and whined and jolted and stuck. Somebody was firing a rifle in a fun booth for cigarette packets and china vases.

'Have you brought a gun, sir?' Crosse asked.

Here Greene is using a highly realistic technique to portray a recognizable landscape and then imbue that landscape with his own moral point of view, so that the West End of London becomes a vivid projection of a state of mind. In other words, we recognize the world on Greene's terms. He also manipulates plot to similar ends, though this tends to undermine the sense of reality we have observed. The number of accidental meetings, for example – Conrad chancing to see the Assistant Commissioner and the private secretary at the beginning of the novel, and Jules bumping into Kay just as she has been stood up by Surrogate (and as they drive off together they pass Conder in the street) – are barely credible. Similarly, the author intrudes on the sense of reality by an abundance of self-conscious irony, as when he allows off-hand remarks to become prophecies: Milly warning Conrad that all his talk will get him is a bed in hospital; the Assistant Commissioner's housekeeper telling him that she's afraid one day she will find him shot down on the doorstep –

which would have happened except for the (also ironical) fact that Conrad's gun is loaded with blanks. Conrad's name is another instance of authorial irony – his parents named him after a Polish seaman who had lodged with them, and about whom they had not noticed anything special (clearly Joseph Conrad, whose *Secret Agent* is the main influence on the book).

It's a Battlefield is Greene's first mature novel, and the skilful way in which he handles an extremely complex plot is a considerable technical achievement. One particularly subtle way in which he draws the different strands of the story together is by the recurrent use of certain images and metaphors. Thus, as we have seen, considerable play is made of the battle leitmotif, so that the story is dominated by imagery reminiscent of a battle fought in fog. Other images are picked up in the same way, uniting the diverse characters involved in the Drover affair. The Assistant Commissioner recalls a piece of evidence in the murder case he is trying to solve:

. . . turning over in [his] mind the woollen béret, noting the texture of the wool, the pattern of the crochet, he understood more than the most sensitive artist, noticed more than the most inquisitive woman.

Later, Milly is crocheting a béret but is unable to read the pattern until Conrad teaches her how. Another leitmotif is the unexplained joke about the pram on a taxi, a chance remark by the private secretary which Conrad overhears; it had confused and worried the Assistant Commissioner, but it infuriates Conrad to see that the men who have Jim's life in their hands should be able to laugh so easily over such an absurdity, and as he tracks down the Assistant Commissioner, determined for revenge, the phrase haunts him, becoming in his mind a symbol of the heartlessness and injustice of authority.

IV

In *A Sort of Life* Greene describes how, at the age of fifteen and on the verge of a nervous breakdown due to the unrelenting misery of the life he endured at school, he made a break for freedom by escaping to Berkhamsted Common, determined 'to remain there until my parents agreed that never again should I go back to my prison'. The plan was foiled, however, when he was discovered by his elder sister Molly: 'I could have run, of course, but that hardly suited the dignity of my protest, and so I went quietly home with her. It was a tactical defeat, but it proved all the same a strategical victory.' This episode changed the direction of his life, 'the whole future was decisively altered', as his parents realized the full extent of his desperate situation and released him from school, sending him instead to a London psychoanalyst.

A similarly decisive moment occurs in Anthony Farrant's life in *England Made Me*. He too ran away from school and was met in a barn by his twin-sister, Kate, who persuaded him to return; this moment shaped his future as it had shaped Greene's, but Anthony was less fortunate, for he returned reluctantly to his prison where nothing had changed, and resigned himself to captivity: 'One even after a time adapted oneself to circumstances, learned the secret of being tolerated, wore with conviction the common uniform.'

The novel begins many years later, when Anthony is a shabby figure in his thirties who has drifted from one failure to another since leaving school. Down on his luck yet again, he is helped by Kate, who through talent and ambition, and a certain amount of ruthlessness, has become a powerful figure in the Krogh empire, based in Stockholm. She persuades Krogh, whose mistress she is, to hire Anthony as a personal bodyguard, thus fulfilling her ambition of having Anthony near her again and of somehow atoning for what she sees as the harm she caused him by persuading him to return to school. When Krogh asks to marry her and offers a settlement for both her and Anthony, she thinks:

I've undone the damage I did when I sent him back, back from the barn to conform, to pick up the conventions, the manners of all the rest. He tried to break away and I sent him back.

England Made Me is, as the title suggests, more than anything a novel about roots and social conditioning. It continues the indictment of modern civilization begun in *It's a Battlefield*, though it is a much more ambitious novel. It goes deeper than the earlier novel's social and political analysis, painting an even more depressing and pessimistic picture of helpless individuals at the mercy of a disordered society and incapable of escaping a determined fate.

Krogh, the rich industrialist (a character based on the match millionaire Ivar Kreugar) represents the new, rootless, international civilization of the twentieth century. This is in contrast to the dying, traditional world of old-fashioned moral values represented by Anthony and the seedy, expatriate journalist Minty. They have both been emotionally crippled by their English public school education, although they still adhere to the values instilled in them by fathers and schoolmasters:

But these were his maxims. Do not show your feelings. Do not love immoderately. Be chaste, prudent, pay your debts. Don't buy on credit . . . Anthony learning (the beating in the nursery, the tears before boarding school) to keep a stiff upper lip, Anthony learning (the beating in the study when he brought home the smutty book with the pretty pictures) that you must honour other men's sisters.

Anthony and Minty's pathetic, bitter and resentful attachment to the old school is further evidence of how their upbringing has damaged them, for they seem arrested in a permanent adolescence, still behaving, and talking, like schoolboys. For example, Minty expresses his dislike of sex and women in terms which must be unique to men educated at a British public school: 'He didn't like girls, he couldn't have said it in words more plainly; tawdry little creatures, other people's sisters, their hats blocking the view at Lord's.'

The old world of traditional moral values and 'the new frontierless world' of cut-throat materialism meet in the character of Kate, who is torn between the two and is likened to 'a tunnel connecting two landscapes':

Her dusty righteous antecedents pulled at her heart, but with all her intellect she claimed alliance with the present, this crooked day, this inhumanity . . .

Although she has severed herself from her roots, Kate maintains a sense of what she has lost:

Deliberately she turned away from the thought that there had been a straightness about the poor national past which the international present did without. It hadn't been very grand, but in their class at any rate there had been gentleness and kindness once.

There is no such kindness in the crooked, chromium-plated present, however, for now it is every man for himself in a battle for survival. There is now no room for ideals or even scruples:

Minty sneered: 'Socialism.' 'Oh no,' Kate said, 'That's not for us. No brotherhood in our boat. Only who can cut the biggest dash and who can swim.'

When Krogh's unscrupulousness crosses the threshold into illegality and his methods show a true streak of evil, it is paradoxically the weak Anthony who takes a moral stand. Although Kate realizes that what Krogh is doing is wrong, she sees only the opportunity to profit from her knowledge. Anthony's gentlemanly sense of decency, on the other hand, finds Krogh's behaviour unacceptable. Kate is aware that Anthony was not only 'all the moral consciousness . . . that they could summon up between them', but also that this moral consciousness is a form of his conventionality, a sign that he is trapped in the old system. Anthony's failure, his weakness and conventionality, becomes then a form of moral triumph as we see that he has never unlearned the strict moral lessons beaten into him at home and at school. By going back from the barn to conform, he was sentenced to a lifetime of adherence to a set of values and standards which, even if he was unable to live up to them, he drew the line at deliberately dishonouring.

Krogh has no such scruples and has no allegiance to the values of the 'older world' he has cut himself off from. He is truly rootless, 'like a man who could only speak Esperanto'. Existence for him has been a process of escaping and betraying everything in his past: 'To live is to leave behind; to be as free as a shipwrecked man who has lost everything.' However, as Krogh perceives, liberating himself from the past has only meant imprisoning himself in the present: 'It left him with a sense of loneliness, of dryness, as if his life were narrower instead of infinitely enlarged.'

In later novels religious faith and human love offer Greene's characters the possibility of relief from the loneliness and the 'dryness', and the possibility of 'enlarging' life, but the only characters in *England Made Me* to experience love are Anthony and Kate, who persistently try to avoid it. During the course of Anthony's time in Stockholm they slowly become aware of their true, incestuous, feelings for each other, but, as Greene explains in *Ways of Escape*, both use 'their superficial sexual loves, Kate with Krogh and Anthony with Loo, to evade the real right thing'.

The nature of Kate's feelings for Anthony is established in the first line of the book, 'She might have been waiting for her lover', and slowly through the course of their reunion they move closer together. Kate is more aware of her sexual desire for him, recalling in a passage of interior monologue that the only sexual satisfaction she had experienced with Krogh was due to her having been aroused by another man with a strong physical resemblance to Anthony. Anthony himself is jealous of Krogh because he is Kate's lover, but distracts himself from his true feelings with meaningless relationships or casual pick-ups, like the actress who sees through him:

> 'Is that your sister?'
> 'Yes.'
> 'I don't believe you. You're in love with her.'
> 'Yes.'
> 'You naughty boy.'

When the 'itch' becomes too strong for him he decides to follow the pathetic Loo back to Coventry. His love for Loo is the love of bland and easy seduction, of *Film Fun* and romantic cliché. For Anthony, love is a good time, not the serious, difficult, bewildering emotion he feels for Kate:

Love was not gratitude, love was not this dependence of the brain, this thought-reading, this inconvenience of shared pain, this was the unfortunate trick of being twins . . .

In the end he understands that this after all is the true form of love: it 'occurred to him with astonishment and pain' and 'he was conscious of a great waste, a great disappointment'. He tries to tell Kate about this 'discovery' of his love for her, but is distracted by Krogh's call, and one is left in doubt as to whether this is true self-discovery on Anthony's part, or just another 'temporary break in the cloud of [his] self-deception'.

Apart from human love, Greene's later characters are also offered religious belief as a way of 'enlarging life'. Here it is only the journalist Minty who has any sense of religion, and this little more than a conformist allegiance to his Anglo-Catholic upbringing. Religion now for him has the same quality as the annual Old Harrovian dinner; it is a form of nostalgic indulgence, a temporary chance of escape. He dives for the open door of a church with 'the dry-mouthed excitement of a secret debauchee' to take in 'the genuine air of plaster images, of ever-burning light, of sins forgiven'. The symbol of Minty's belief, and of his life, is the spider he keeps trapped under his toothglass. This represents a depressingly deterministic view of life, in which man cannot rise to help himself and has no opportunity to exercise free will or to evolve. Finishing his prayers ('that God would cast down the mighty from their seats and exalt the humble and meek, that he would give Minty his daily bread . . . and growing more particular, that Anthony . . .') he turns out the light and waits patiently for sleep:

And like the spider he withered, blown out no longer to meet contempt; his body stretched doggo in the attitude of death, he lay there humbly tempting God to lift the glass.

All the characters are trapped, like Minty. Even Krogh, who has broken away from his past, is locked behind the glass walls of his self-made prison, the great cube of glass and steel. Krogh wants to break away, to be as free as a shipwrecked man (*Shipwrecks* was the original pre-publication title Greene chose for the story). But the depressing conclusion is that it is impossible to break free – man is a trapped creature.

2 Entertainments:
The World Remade by William Le Queux

I

Greene originally called his thrillers 'entertainments', to distinguish them from the more serious 'novels', and it was his ability to excite readers and create a convincing atmosphere of danger and suspense in these 'entertainments' that first won him the enormous popular following that has remained faithful ever since. The 'entertainments' (*Stamboul Train, The Confidential Agent, A Gun for Sale, The Ministry of Fear*, and *Our Man in Havana*) are distinct from the 'novels' mainly in that they place greater emphasis on surface action than on thematic content. However, there is a strong vein of seriousness in all of Greene's work so that even in the entertainments action serves as bait on the moral hook. As Greene said in an interview in 1969: 'If you excite your audience first, you can put over what you will of horror, suffering, truth.'

Greene's decision to write another thriller in 1935 was made partly because of a need to earn money after the relative commercial failures of *It's a Battlefield* and *England Made Me*, but also because of a long-felt desire to write a melodrama in the manner of John Buchan. However, Greene realized that the moral climate during the Depression was no place for a Buchan hero ('it was no longer a Buchan world') so that the hunted man of *A Gun for Sale* is Raven, not Hannay: 'a man out to revenge himself for all the dirty tricks of life, not to save his country' (*WE*).

The plot of *A Gun for Sale* is a neatly arranged assembly of coincidence, irony and melodrama. Sir Marcus, a millionaire armaments manufacturer, hires Raven, a ruthless criminal with 'a splinter of ice in his heart', to murder the idealistic War Minister of a foreign government. The assassination brings

Europe to the brink of war and raises the 'consumption of munitions' to 'several million pounds a day', thus creating magnificent profits for Sir Marcus.

Raven is not a truly evil person, for he is seen as the victim of sociological and psychological forces beyond his control. On the other hand, Sir Marcus and his agent Davis represent the ultimate evil of unscrupulous capitalists prepared to kill and destroy for personal profit. They even cheat Raven by paying him with stolen banknotes (it is for passing these that Raven attracts the attention of the police). Furious at being double-crossed, Raven determines to revenge himself on them and thus an ironic double hunt begins: to the detective, Mather, it seems 'petty', 'chasing down a small thief' (the possessor of the stolen banknotes) and he wishes instead that he had a chance to go after a really important criminal like the Minister's assassin, not knowing of course that they are one and the same person. Meanwhile, Raven himself is in pursuit of personal 'justice', hunting down Davis and Sir Marcus. The ironies increase when Raven takes Mather's girlfriend, Anne, as a hostage to help him escape from the police. The local constabulary in Nottwich, the town Raven runs to in pursuit of his corrupt employers, assume that Anne is his accomplice, and Mather is persuaded to believe this too. Thus, while Anne thinks Mather is trying to rescue her, he is in fact trying to catch her, and she, rather than assisting Raven's escape, as the police believe, is ultimately responsible for his arrest.

In the wartime essay 'At Home', Greene wrote that after years of the threat of war and the expectation of violence on a universal scale, life in the blitzed cities seemed 'just and poetic', for it had become, with the final breaking of 'an old dog-toothed civilization', what 'it ought to be':

Violence comes to us more easily because it was so long expected – not only by the political sense but by the moral sense. The world we lived in could not have ended any other way. The curious waste lands one sometimes saw from trains – the crated ground round Wolverhampton under a cindery sky with a few cottages grouped like stoves among the rubbish: those acres of abandoned cars round Slough: the dingy fortune-teller's on the first floor above the cheap permanent waves in Brighton back streets: they all demanded violence, like the rooms in a dream where one knows that something will presently happen – a door fly open or a window-catch give and let the end in.

It is in this atmosphere of expectation that *A Gun for Sale* takes place. The characters are obsessed by the threat of war. They are bombarded with newspaper headlines, electric news signs, radio broadcasts – all building up the sense of expectation to such a degree that Samuel Hynes in *The Auden Generation* describes the book as 'a war-novel before the event'.

As in *It's a Battlefield*, the 'private struggle' of the individual is contrasted, and related, to the wider political struggle of mass society in which the individual is an insignificant and impotent unit. War is seen as bringing this tension to crisis point, affecting as it does everyone in society. Different individuals, however, relate to the idea of war in different ways. Raven, the 'sour, bitter' murderer who 'had been made by hatred', is directly responsible for bringing Europe to the brink of war by his murder of the Minister, yet for him war makes no difference, 'it was normality he couldn't cope with': 'All this talk of war. It doesn't mean a thing to me. Why should I care if there's a war? There's always been a war for me.'

Sir Marcus and Davis welcome the expected war, but they are not alone in this. Buddy, the medical student, is a natural leader of men, and so expects to be a war hero, which will save him from 'the confinements, the provincial practice, the one dull wife and the bridge parties'. However, when his courage is truly tested, by Raven's forcing him at gunpoint into the garage and ordering him to strip, it fails him. The hard reality of modern war, the humiliation of being dominated by this 'mean, thin, undernourished city rat, whose arm he could have snapped with a single twist', destroys his adolescent dreams. His friends never understood the change this brought about in him, but

. . . they had not looked forward with pleasure and excitement to war, they hadn't been Buddy, the daredevil of the trenches one minute, before genuine war in the shape of an automatic in a thin desperate hand pressed on him.

For the rest of society war is something of a dream, too, until Raven's murder of the Minister brings reality crashing in on them. When Anne joins the crowd watching the electric news sign in the street, she is shocked that there is no cheering or flag-waving, only silence and fear. She then sets out to stop the impending war, by assisting the police in their capture of Raven. But she realizes that it is only a temporary respite because 'men were fighting beasts, they needed war'. The 'ultimatum' is already off the front page and as she looks at the paper and out of the train window it seems to be Greene himself speaking, the Greene of *Journey Without Maps* and 'At Home':

It was no longer on the front page, but that was only because to Nottwich readers there was a war nearer at hand, fought out to a finish in the Tanneries. How they love it, she thought bitterly, as the dusk came up from the dark wounded ground and the glow of furnaces became visible beyond the long black ridge of slag-heaps. This was war too: this chaos through which the train moved slowly, grinding over point after point like a dying creature dragging itself painfully away through No-Man's Land from the scene of battle.

In Greene's portrait of contemporary England the landscape itself seems infected with the 'seediness' which has become a part of everyone's lives. It is an extremely subjective portrait, made up of those aspects of the landscape and the townscape which correspond to Greene's own 'mindscape', a view of the world which pervades his fictional creation so strongly that some critics say he is describing not real life but a mythical 'Greeneland'. Anne's view from the train in the passage above gives some credence to this idea, as does the following description of the new housing estate to which Raven takes her at gunpoint:

They had left the little dirty houses behind them. She read the name of the new street: Shakespeare Avenue. Bright-red bricks and tudor gables and half timbering, doors with stained glass, names like Restholme. These houses represented something worse than the meanness of poverty, the meanness of the spirit . . . It occurred to Anne that he had brought her here to kill her in the scarred fields behind the housing estate, where the grass had been trampled into the clay and the stumps of trees showed where an old wood had been.

Although we are supposed to be seeing the scene through Anne's eyes, the terms 'meanness of spirit' and 'scarred fields', and the whole tone of the description, seem out of character: this is not Anne looking at the estate but the author, and it is more than an expression of simple distaste for the new forms of housing development and the ersatz architecture of suburbia, however horrific they may be. Greene is appalled by the soullessness and despair, a despair emphasized by the drab 'scarred fields' and the gentle irony of the names – 'Shakespeare Avenue', 'Restholme'. It is the spiritual wasteland behind the literal wasteland that Greene is drawing his reader's attention to.

II

After *A Gun for Sale*, Greene wrote *Brighton Rock*, the best of his thrillers. However, it is more complex and problematic than the entertainments we are concerned with here, and is therefore dealt with in the following chapter.

Greene's next 'entertainment' was *The Confidential Agent*, which he finished in six weeks in 1938 out of a desperate need to earn money for his family in case he was called up for armed service. He wrote it in the mornings and spent the afternoons working much more slowly and laboriously on *The Power and the Glory*, sustained all the while by doses of Benzedrine. This perhaps explains why *The Confidential Agent* is not of the same calibre as the other entertainments of the period, *A Gun for Sale* and *The Ministry of Fear*. It is, nevertheless, a highly readable novel and one of the few of his books Greene himself still cares to re-read:

. . . perhaps because it is not really one of mine. It was as though I were ghosting for another man. D, the chivalrous agent and professor of Romance literature, is not really one of my characters . . .
(*WE*)

Like *A Gun for Sale*, *The Confidential Agent* is concerned with trust and loyalty in the extreme situation of war. The agent of the title is D, who comes to England to purchase essential supplies of coal for his government which is engaged in a bitter civil war (the government remains unnamed, but this clearly refers to the Spanish Civil War). The opposition also send an agent to buy the same supply of coal, and whoever obtains the coal will gain a decisive advantage over the other side.

The title itself is ironic. D's government has no 'confidence' in him, and he no longer has any confidence in himself, nor does he trust anyone else. In the severe testing ground of a war men are seen to be too concerned for their own fates, and human nature seen to be too weak, to remain unquestionably loyal to a cause or a particular side. D's own motives for remaining loyal to Communism, and for working as a secret agent for the cause, have the ring of psychological authenticity. One must choose a side, he explains, 'once and for all', and stick to it, not because it is necessarily the right side ('only history can tell that') but because without belief in something life would be intolerable:

'You've got to choose some line of action and live by it. Otherwise nothing matters at all. You probably end with a gas-oven. I've chosen certain people who've had the lean portion for some centuries now . . . You might say it's the only job left for anyone – sticking to a job. It's no good taking a moral line. My people commit atrocities like the others. I suppose if I believed in a god it would be simpler.'

D carries his sense of distrust with him to England, which here is no longer described in terms of war, as in *It's a Battlefield* and *A Gun for Sale*. For D, who has come from the real war, it is 'peaceful and preoccupied', and he is amazed by the calmness of its people, who are so unaware of the war that he is bringing to their shores, infecting their peace. But soon he realizes that beneath the veneer of peace is raging the private war of the individual, struggling with life in a world without God – a struggle that is an integral part of the human situation in whatever part of the world. This is emphasized by the anonymity of the agents, for by calling them D and L Greene avoids localizing a universal malaise:

He had imagined that the suspicion which was the atmosphere of his own life was due to civil war, but he began to believe that it existed everywhere: it was part of human life . . . He had been too absorbed in the old days with his love and with the Berne Ms. and the weekly lecture on Romance Languages to notice it. It was as if the whole world lay in the shadow of abandonment.

III

In 1941 Greene returned to West Africa, this time as an agent for MI6 – an episode described vividly in *Ways of Escape*. On the voyage there he was inspired by a 'fantastic and funny' detective story by Michael Innes, and thus he began to write what he intended to be a funny and fantastic thriller. The result was *The Ministry of Fear*, one of the best entertainments, yet, despite a certain grim irony in the twists and turns of the plot, a decidedly unfunny book.

Perhaps it was the circumstances of the time – December 1941, Japan had just struck at Pearl Harbor, the German armies were smashing their way towards Moscow – we listened every night to the news on the steward's radio – that made the plot I chose for *The Ministry of Fear* seem to me a funny one . . .
(*WE*)

Set against the dramatic background of London in the Blitz, the story tells how Rowe, an unadventurous man more or less detached from the chaos and violence, becomes involved in a strange and sinister underworld when he innocently gives a secret password – by guessing the correct weight of a cake at a charity fête. The mysterious organization whose illegal plans he has inadvertently sabotaged makes several attempts to retrieve the cake, which conceals a secret (never revealed to Rowe or the reader). Rowe manages to fight them off until suddenly a bomb strikes his home. He is knocked unconscious, and as a consequence loses his memory. When he comes to, he finds himself an amnesia patient called Digby in a nursing home run by a Dr Forester who, it turns out, is involved in the plot against him.

Before he lost his memory Rowe had been burdened with guilt for having murdered his terminally ill wife. It was a mercy killing, done out of a sense of pity, but exactly whom he was having pity

on is in doubt, for it was he who had been unable to bear his
wife's pain – and not she. Pity is one of the central themes of *The
Ministry of Fear*, a theme which Greene was later to explore in
greater depth in the character of Scobie in *The Heart of the
Matter*. It is seen here as a monstrous sentiment, variously called
'dangerous', 'more promiscuous than lust', 'horrible and horrify-
ing', and 'the worst passion'. Pity assumes a superiority over the
person pitied and 'from that eminence', as W. H. Auden
observed when reviewing the book in *Renascence*, 'the step to the
torture chamber and the corrective labour camp is shorter than
one thinks'. Auden calls pity 'the heresy of our time' and it is, in
a more strictly religious sense, a heretical sentiment for it leads
one to assume responsibility for other people's existence, which
implies a lack of trust in God. Rowe has lost his sense of God,
but for Scobie, the Catholic in *The Heart of the Matter*, the
dilemma is made much more difficult because Catholics 'know all
the answers': as always in Greene's fiction, faith complicates life,
rather than simplifies it.

The paradox of pity, however, is that it is a vice born out of
love, so that according to Anna, the girl with whom 'Digby' falls
in love, it is only people who do not care who are not prone to it
(a conclusion reached by another man of pity, Conrad in *It's a
Battlefield*). Their sense of pity also leads Rowe and Scobie to
become victims themselves, not of self-pity, as Auden suggests,
but of the more extreme emotion of despair.

The Ministry of Fear is also the entertainment most concerned
with another of Greene's main themes, the lost innocence of
childhood. It is nostalgia for this lost innocence which draws
Rowe to the fête at the start of the book, and it is one of the finer
ironies of the story that his visit to a lost world of security is what
drags him into the modern, adult chaos of politics and violence.
Childhood means for Rowe a time of simplicity and faith, when

heaven is as near and actual as the seaside . . . God is good, the grown-
up man or woman knows the answer to every question, there is such a
thing as truth . . .

The symbol of this lost innocence is a children's historical
romance called *The Little Duke*, by the best-selling Victorian
novelist Charlotte M. Yonge. Rowe remembers it from his own

childhood and when he comes across a second-hand copy at the fête he buys it for sixpence with 'an ache of the heart', and Greene uses phrases from it as epigraphs for each chapter. Rowe finds the books of childhood more satisfying than adult books, for they 'promised a world of great simplicity of which we knew the rules, but the later books are complicated and contradictory with experience . . .' In this, the adult world, the little Duke 'is dead and betrayed and forgotten'.

As he walks round the fête, Rowe wishes 'to mislay the events of twenty years' and this, ironically, is exactly what does happen to him later when he loses his memory during the explosion and finds himself in Dr Forester's nursing home. The episodes in the nursing home are told mainly from Rowe's point of view. He feels secure in the hands of the staff and lives in happy ignorance of the sort of person he really is. Life is once again simple, there is such a thing as good and evil and there is an 'adult', the doctor, who takes charge and who 'knows the answer to every question'. The passages in which Rowe tries to guess what he 'does' in life are full of ironic pathos as he recalls the heroic ambitions of his boyhood and feels sure that somehow he has lived up to them. However, he is disturbed by the sudden vague remembrance of a rat (the first victim of his pity):

'. . . I did want to be an explorer – but that's unlikely. Even with this beard. They tell me the beard really does belong. I wouldn't know. Oh,' he went on, 'I had enormous dreams of discovering unknown tribes in Central Africa. Medicine? No, I never liked doctoring. Too much pain. I hated pain.' He was troubled by a slight dizziness. He said, 'It made me feel ill, sick, hearing of pain. I remember – something about a rat.'

The man has become a child again, temporarily, but 'the child does make the man', and is equally corrupted by pity: it was as a child that Rowe first learned about pain, as a child he killed the injured rat because he could not bear to witness its suffering.

In the clinic is a green baize door leading to the sick bay. With its barred windows and high wall, this is a place of fear for the patients who know that 'hysteria over a game', or 'tears that came too quickly', could lead to the straitjacket and removal to one of its padded cells. Rowe doubts if anyone is actually in the dreaded sick bay. It is, he thinks, like 'the conception of Hell presented by sympathetic theologians – a place without inhabitants which existed simply as a warning'. This view changes when Major Stone, a fellow patient, is suddenly taken off there and Rowe threatened, by the now tyrannical-seeming Forester, with the same fate. Then, remembering a similar action as a child, Rowe decides to go through the green baize door at night and talk to Stone. When he was a boy, Greene's home and school were separated by a green baize door leading from his father's study. The door divided the two worlds of innocence and experience: on one side was the civilization of home; on the other lurked 'a savage country of strange customs and inexplicable cruelties'. Rowe goes through the door of the clinic with a sense of childhood adventure and heroics and, like Greene, re-enters the bewildering chaos of adulthood.

In his essay 'The Last Buchan', Greene wrote that 'certainly we can all see now "how thin is the protection of civilization" '. Buchan had shown this by making adventures happen in familiar surroundings to unadventurous men, and it was a fictional device Greene himself imitated. In all Greene's thrillers 'normal', uninvolved people, such as Rose in *The Confidential Agent*, Anne in *A Gun for Sale*, Rowe in *The Ministry of Fear*, are 'reluctant heroes', sucked unwillingly into the whirlpool of politics, crime and violence. The panic they experience on finding themselves dragged into this chaos is described by Rowe in an imaginary conversation with his dead mother:

It sounds like a thriller, doesn't it, but the thrillers are like life – more like life than you are, this lawn, your sandwiches, that pine. You used to laugh at the books Miss Savage read – about spies, and murders, and violence, and wild motor-car chases, but dear, that's real life: it's what we've all made of the world since you died. I'm your little Arthur who wouldn't hurt a beetle and I'm a murderer too. The world has been remade by William Le Queux.

IV

During almost his entire career Greene has had close associations with the cinema. More of his work has been translated to film than that of any other major modern novelist, and for four and a half years before the war he reviewed films weekly in *The Spectator* and *Night and Day*, laying claim to be one of the most influential British film critics ever.

He has also written a number of original screenplays, most notably *The Third Man* and *The Fallen Idol*. However, before these, in the 1940s, he wrote a treatment for a film that was never made. The treatment, called *The Tenth Man*, was finally published in 1985 amid a great deal of publicity, for Greene himself had forgotten about it and the manuscript came to light only when it was sold to an American publisher by MGM, who own the rights.

The plot of *The Tenth Man* is complicated and far-fetched. Chavel, a French prisoner-of-war who in normal life is a rich lawyer, is chosen as one of ten men whom the German soldiers will execute as a reprisal for Resistance attacks. Unlike the other nine, Chavel is unable to meet death coolly, and persuades Janvier, a fellow prisoner, to face the firing squad in his place in exchange for his house in the country and all his wealth. Janvier agrees to this bargain in order to provide for his mother and sister and to fulfil a dream of dying a rich man. It is a deal that earns Chavel the hatred and contempt of the other prisoners and after his release he returns, humiliated and destitute, to his estate. There he finds Janvier's Miss Haversham-like mother and his sister Thérèse, who is full of hatred for Chavel and lives in hope of one day taking revenge on him. He gives his name as 'Charlot' and she employs him as an odd-job man and, ironically, as a lookout for Chavel, for he claims to have known Chavel and she wants someone who will be able to recognize him if he appears so that she can spit in his face. As irony is heaped on irony, a con-man arrives at the house claiming to be Chavel and the story ends with the real Chavel, who has fallen in love with Thérèse, trying to prove to her that he is Chavel, the man she hates, and that the other man is an impostor.

Although somewhat sketchily and loosely written, *The Tenth Man* is extremely evocative of certain atmospheres: particularly the mixture of fear and boredom in the prison scenes and the sense of exhaustion and hopelessness of people reeling from the effects of war. It is the story of a whole society of 'reluctant heroes' whose lives are dominated by international politics, a society in which disguise and impersonation are made easy because of the

toll taken on everyone's faces by the war: after six years of
suffering everyone's passport photograph is out of date. Greene
is presenting here a different view of the effect of war on society
from the one presented earlier in *The Ministry of Fear*, where
even the Blitz is described in almost festive terms (the flares
above Rowe came 'sailing slowly, beautifully, down, like clusters
of spangles off a Christmas tree') and people walk around with
cheerful faces, as if it were a national holiday.

Many of Greene's major themes are incorporated into the
story in miniature, as it were: betrayal, forgiveness, the moment
of weakness or cowardice 'which happens to everyone once' and
'when it happens, you know what you've been all your life'. It is
also, like *The Ministry of Fear*, the story of a man changing his
identity: Rowe loses his memory, becomes Digby and is in fact a
changed character: 'He was Arthur Rowe with a difference', 'He
was next door to his own youth: he had started again from there.'
Chavel in *The Tenth Man* becomes Charlot and he, too, has the
chance to start again through humiliation, destitution, and through
his love for Thérèse.

Although *The Tenth Man* may yet prove to be an excellent
film, in printed form it is a disappointment. The fact that it is
written in story form at all, rather than as a screenplay, is a
technical matter:

A film depends on a certain measure of characterization, on mood and
atmosphere, and these seem impossible to capture for the first time in
the dull shorthand of a conventional treatment.
(*WE*)

Greene's most successful screenplays are two he wrote for the
English director, Carol Reed: *The Fallen Idol*, a dramatization of
his own short story 'The Basement Room' (discussed in Chapter
Three), and *The Third Man*. In the latter, probably the best
known of all his stories, Rollo Martin searches for his friend
Harry Lime (played by Orson Welles) after Lime's mock funeral
in Vienna, and discovers that Lime is really a black-marketeer
dealing in penicillin. Like *The Tenth Man*, the story was never
intended to be read and as literature is unexciting, simply the bare
bones of a story which came vividly to life in the cinema, becoming
one of the most popular and successful films of all time.

3 Short Stories:
Through the Green Baize Door

Although a prolific writer of short stories, Greene insists that he is nevertheless 'a novelist who has happened to write short stories, just as there are certain short-story writers (Maupassant and Victor Pritchett come to mind) who have happened to write novels' (*WE*). The distinction between the two sorts of writers is not just a question of technique, as it might be between an artist who works in oils and another who works in watercolours. It is, Greene claims, the distinction between 'two different ways of life', and for him the short story has always been yet another 'way of escape': '. . . Escape from having to live with a character for years on end, picking up his jealousies, his meanness, his dishonest tricks of thought, his betrayals' (*WE*).

Greene's comments on these different ways of life lead him to an interesting conclusion on the artistic purity of the short story, as compared to the novel:

With a novel, which takes perhaps years to write, the author is not the same man at the end of the book as he was at the beginning. It is not only that his characters have developed – he has developed with them, and this nearly always gives a sense of roughness to the work: a novel can seldom have the sense of perfection which you find in Chekhov's story, 'The Lady with the Dog'.
(*WE*)

Greene's early stories are considerably less ambitious than his early novels – not only in length, but in depth of character, analysis of motive, and in 'message'. This is presumably because he took them less seriously, considering them as 'escapes' or 'scraps', but, paradoxically, it is thanks to this absence of apprentice ambitiousness that some of his best early writing is to be found in the stories. 'I Spy' (1929), for example, is without any of the painfully laboured stylistics which mar *The Name of Action* and *Rumour at Nightfall*. In this story a boy creeps downstairs at night and enters his father's shop to steal his first taste of tobacco. While there he sees his father with two mysterious strangers, who turn out to be policemen (we assume this from their refusal to smoke 'on duty'). They then take the father away and the boy is left with a sense of loneliness and abandonment. It is an uncomplicated, short, open-ended tale, but Greene manages to achieve in it what he so badly failed to achieve in the novels of the same period. He evokes a genuine atmosphere of mystery and tension, and through the use of simple, straightforward language makes the action exciting. Gone are the laborious descriptions, the endless delving into motive, the lifeless dialogue we find in *The Name of Action* and *Rumour at Nightfall*:

But as he moved he heard footfalls in the street, the sound of several men walking rapidly. Charlie Stowe was old enough to feel surprise that anybody was about. The footsteps came nearer, stopped; a key was turned in the shop door, a voice said: 'Let him in,' and then he heard his father, 'If you wouldn't mind being quiet, gentlemen. I don't want to wake up the family.' There was a note unfamiliar to Charlie in the undecided voice. A torch flashed and the electric globe burst into blue light. The boy held his breath; he wondered whether his father would hear his heart beating, and he clutched his night-shirt tightly and prayed, 'O God, don't let me be caught'. Through a crack in the counter he could see his father where he stood, one hand held to his high stiff collar, between two men in bowler hats and belted mackintoshes. They were strangers.

Greene's early stories were collected in *Nineteen Stories* (1947). This was later revised as *Twenty-One Stories* (1954) in which two stories were withdrawn ('The Lottery Ticket' and 'The Other Side of the Border') and four new stories added: 'The Hint of an Explanation', 'The Blue Film', 'Special Duties' and 'The Destructors'. The next collection of stories to be published was *A Sense of Reality* (1963) – a somewhat ironic title, for in two of the four stories contained in the book – 'Under the Garden' and 'A Discovery in the Woods' – Greene introduces elements of dream and fantasy into his world, questioning traditional perceptions of reality. The stories in *A Sense of Reality* are among Greene's best, particularly 'A Visit to Morin', the account of a Catholic writer's loss of faith (discussed in Chapter Four), and 'Under the Garden', the 'great traveller' Wilditch's re-exploration of his childhood fantasies. The last volume of stories published by Greene is *May We Borrow Your Husband* (1967). This is a collection of short 'comedies of the sexual act' which are slick, cynical, and disappointingly slight compared to the intense power of *A Sense of Reality*.

Although the range of characters and subjects dealt with in the short stories is extremely broad, there is one recurring theme – childhood – which dominates every collection as Greene returns to it again and again, examining it from many different angles. In particular, Greene is interested in those moments in childhood where there is a transition from innocence to experience – moments in which characters and destinies are formed, and the future is 'let in', as he says on several occasions. These 'transition stories' can be separated into two categories. Firstly, there are stories such as 'I Spy', 'The End of the Party', 'The Basement Room', 'The Destructors' and 'A Discovery in the Woods', which are a direct account of childhood experience told from a child's point of view. These are all written in the third person. Secondly there are stories like 'The Hint of an Explanation', 'The Innocent' and 'Under the Garden', in which childhood is revisited and explored, in the first person, from the point of view of an adult.

In 'The Basement Room' (1936), seven-year-old Philip Lane is left alone with the servants when his parents go away. At first he is excited by the prospect of freedom; he cannot wait to go through the green baize door to the servants quarters and 'begin to live'. As in *The Ministry of Fear* and the account of Greene's own childhood in *A Sort of Life*, the green baize door separates the innocence and security of childhood from the confusing, hostile wilderness of adulthood (see Introduction, page 13):

Philip Lane went downstairs and pushed at the baize door; he looked into the pantry, but Baines was not there, then he set foot for the first time on the stairs to the basement. Again he had the sense: this is life. All his seven nursery years vibrated with the strange, the new experience.

Philip's enthusiasm for 'life' soon turns to fear as he discovers the realities of the grown-up world: the hatred between Baines and his wife, Baines's desperate bid for happiness with his mistress, Emmy, and the lies this involves both he and Philip in after Philip has discovered them together. The story ends with Baines killing his wife, watched by Philip, whose whole life changes in that moment. Having gone through the green baize door to find himself 'caught up in other people's darkness', Philip finds he cannot return to the innocence of the nursery world, which has now been lost for ever. Experience has been forced upon him and he cannot escape it: 'The whole house had been turned over to the grown-up world; he wasn't safe in the night nursery; their passions had flooded in.'

The trauma of the moment makes Philip retreat into himself. He 'surrenders responsibility once and for all' and becomes incapable of the adult love or hate which has overwhelmed him: 'That was what happened when you loved – you got involved; and Philip extricated himself from life, from love, from Baines.'

Unlike Philip, the boys of the Wormsley Common Gang in 'The Destructors' (1954) make the transition from innocence to experience of their own free will, as they move from the relatively innocent delinquency of snatching free rides on buses to the senseless destruction of an old man's house. The Gang meets in an 'impromptu car-park, the site of the last bomb in the first blitz', and the war is never far away as a constant reminder of man's instinct for violence, which is the main theme of the story.

Old Misery's house had miraculously escaped destruction in the wartime bombing:

On one side of the car-park leant the first occupied house, No 3, of the shattered Northwood Terrace – literally leant, for it had suffered from the blast of the bomb and the side walls were supported on wooden struts. A smaller bomb and incendiaries had fallen beyond, so that the house stuck up like a jagged tooth and carried on the further wall relics of its neighbour, a dado, the remains of a fireplace.

The leaning house becomes a symbol in the story of precarious peace. Old Misery rests secure in the house, confident that having escaped the destruction of the Blitz it is now safe, not knowing that the Gang, led by the strange newcomer called T, has decided to destroy it. Their apparently fantastic plan is to eat away at the house 'like worms'. They begin by destroying everything inside – opening the pillows and mattresses and tearing up all the paper they can find – as if this were an essential first step to the destruction of the house itself. They then work on the actual structure, sawing through joists and digging out the masonry between the bricks. Before they finish, Old Misery makes a surprise return and they manhandle him into the outside lavatory, where they lock him up overnight in order to complete their work. They cut through the wooden struts on the outside of the house, then attach one end of a rope to the strut and the other to a lorry parked in the car-park. In the morning when the lorry moves off, it pulls the house down.

There is no recognizable motive for the boys' destructiveness. Blackie, the deposed leader, thinks that T's plan must originate in a deep hatred of the old man: ' "Of course I don't hate him", T said. "There'd be no fun if I hated him." ' The violence is senseless, and instinctive. The message here is that the war may be over, but there is no end to the violence. Despite the destruction of whole countries and the loss of millions of lives, mankind has learned nothing, and violence is still an intrinsic part of human nature. There is an echo here of *A Gun for Sale*, in which a European war is narrowly avoided but the expression of violence continues in everyday life, for it is an essential part of the human condition (see page 46).

'The Destructors' is one of Greene's best stories, and his evocation of the child's world, particularly in the wrangling for power within the Gang and the obsession with loyalty among its members, is entirely convincing. On another level, there is a delight in the absurd ironies of the situation. Old Misery has been worried all day since his horoscope in the paper that morning had warned him that he was in danger of a 'serious crash'. 'That might be on this path', he says innocently to T, who is luring him towards the outside lavatory. The fact that the house had escaped the destruction of the German bombing only to be eaten away by a gang of boys is also seen as funny. The lorry driver responsible for the final crash bursts out laughing, much to the fury of Old Misery:

'I'm sorry', the driver said, making heroic efforts, but when he remembered the sudden check of his lorry, the crash of bricks falling, he became convulsed again. One moment the house had stood there with such dignity between the bombsites like a man in a top hat, and then, bang, crash, there wasn't anything left – not anything. He said, 'I'm sorry. I can't help it, Mr Thomas. There's nothing personal, but you got to admit it's funny'.

The same black humour runs throughout almost all the short stories, in which Greene delights in irony, absurdity and quirky, even fantastic twists of fate, which often give the stories an unexpected ending.

'The Innocent' (1937), the first of the stories to deal with childhood from an adult point of view, is a sensitive portrayal of a man's nostalgia for the lost innocence of his boyhood. The story itself is extremely simple. An unnamed first-person narrator takes a casual date on a nostalgic visit to his home town, hoping to recapture a sense of his youth. He tries, as it were, to look back through the green baize door and catch a glimpse of a lost innocence. Because of his companion, his reflections concentrate inevitably on a lost sexual innocence. He remembers how, as a romantic and innocent young boy, he had left 'some passionate message' for a girl in a secret hiding hole. Quite fantastically, he discovers the scrap of paper still there thirty years later. However, what he finds on the paper betrays his sentimental memory: 'All I could remember was the purity, the intensity, the pain of that passion'. What he actually finds on the paper is the drawing of a naked man with a naked woman, which 'might have been drawn by a dirty-minded stranger on a lavatory wall'. Although at first he feels 'betrayed', he gradually begins to realize that what now seems to him vulgarity was in reality an expression of innocence:

. . . later that night, when Lola turned away from me and fell asleep, I began to realize the deep innocence of that drawing. I had believed I was drawing something with a meaning and beautiful: it was only now after thirty years of life that the picture seemed obscene.

In 'The Hint of an Explanation' (1948) two strangers on a train get into conversation about God and the unknown. The narrator is an agnostic, the other a Catholic, and the spiritual uncertainty they express in their conversation is symbolically paralleled by the numerous references to darkness, particularly at the beginning of the story: 'The lights went out entirely in the frequent Pennine tunnels and were too dim anyway for us to read our books . . .'

Greene chooses particular moments for these sudden plunges into darkness, so that he creates not only an atmosphere of unexpected intimacy, freeing the men to talk as in the usual 'two strangers on a train' story, but he gives the darkness a thematic significance similar to that in Conrad's *Heart of Darkness*, where it is used as a symbol for both spiritual ignorance and human evil. In the following passage the two strangers look for 'hints' to explain the nature of human good and evil, and as they do so they are plunged into darkness:

'Of course there is no answer here. We catch hints . . .' and then the train roared into another tunnel and the lights again went out. It was the longest tunnel yet . . . When we emerged into the mere grey of night and the globe lit up once more, I could see that my companion was leaning back on his seat.

I repeated his last word as a question, 'Hints?'

'Oh, they mean very little in cold print – or cold speech,' he said, shivering in his overcoat. 'And they mean nothing at all to another human being than the man who catches them. They are not scientific evidence – or evidence at all for that matter. Events that don't, somehow, turn out as they were intended – by the human actors, I mean, or by the thing behind the human actors.'

'The thing?'

'The word Satan is so anthropomorphic . . .'

The Catholic traveller's 'hint of an explanation' is also that moment which 'let the future in' for him as a child. Growing up in a Catholic family in a largely Protestant society, he had as a boy felt isolated and different. People in the town had taunted him, calling him 'Popey Martin'. Blacker, the town baker and an atheist, had a particularly deep hatred of Catholicism:

That poor man was preparing to revenge himself on everything he hated – my father, the Catholics, the God whom people persisted in crediting – by corrupting me. He had evolved a horrible and ingenious plan.

Blacker's plan is to 'seduce' Popey Martin, by offering him a toy train-set if in exchange he procures for him a consecrated host, which he needs to prove to himself that there is no such thing as transubstantiation. He also threatens to 'bleed' the boy with a razor if he does not comply with his demand. That Sunday at Mass the boy duly removes the host from his own mouth and keeps it for the baker. However, as he lies in bed that night, waiting for Blacker, Popey Martin begins to realize the awesome implications of the sacrilege he has been asked to commit and becomes aware, for the first time, of the forces of good and evil at work in the world:

The Host had always been to me – well, the Host. I knew theoretically, as I have said, what I had to believe, but suddenly, as someone whistled in the road outside, whistled secretively, knowingly, to me, I knew that this which I had beside my bed was something of infinite value – something a man would pay for with his whole peace of mind, something that was so hated one could love it as one loves an outcast or a bullied child. These are adult words and it was a child of ten who lay scared in bed, listening to the whistle from the road, Blacker's whistle, but I think he felt fairly clearly what I am describing now.

Blacker's plan then misfires badly. The boy eats the host on impulse and the atheist begins to cry. Looking back on the moment from his adult point of view, Popey Martin feels that these tears were wept by the forces of evil (what he calls 'the Thing') who controlled the baker:

When I think of it now, it's almost as if I had seen that Thing weeping for its inevitable defeat. It had tried to use me as a weapon and now I had broken in its hands and it wept its hopeless tears through one of Blacker's eyes.

The failure of 'the Thing' takes on its full implications when, at the very end of the story, the coat of the 'stranger' falls open to reveal the collar of a priest. The moment in which he had resisted Blacker's plan to corrupt him had 'let in' a future of service to God and the forces of good. The paradox of this victory comes in the last line when he admits he in fact 'owes a lot' to Blacker: ' "You see, I am a very happy man".'

'Under the Garden' is the longest of all Greene's short stories and, with its blend of reality and fantasy, is quite unlike anything else he has written. Like the Catholic in 'The Hint of an Explanation', the ceaseless traveller Wilditch looks back to his childhood in the hope of finding some sort of explanation of his life. The story is divided into three parts. Parts One and Three are written in the third person and deal with the present; Part Two is Wilditch's own written account of a childhood 'adventure' which he believes has in some way coloured his whole life, but which until now has bewildered him. In fact, the experience was so fantastic he doubts whether it could really have happened at all, and wonders instead whether it had only been a dream.

In Part One Wilditch is informed that he is suffering from a terminal illness, and the dialogue between him and his doctors is laden with irony and pathos. The doctors combine extreme diffidence with extreme insensitivity, so that Sir Nigel, the surgeon, cannot bring himself to tell Wilditch outright that he has cancer, but implies it with some rather brutal hints:

'Have to meet my wife at Liverpool Street [Sir Nigel said]. Are *you* married?'
'No.'
'Oh well, one care the less.'

Wilditch compares the surgeon to a fisherman, playing his line with cunning and patience so that he finally 'hooks' Wilditch into awareness:

'Ah yes,' Sir Nigel said. 'Any brothers or sisters? You, I mean.'
'An elder brother. Why?'
'Oh well, I suppose it's all on the record,' Sir Nigel said, rolling in his line.

Having at last taken in the fact that he is dying, Wilditch decides to pay a final visit to the house where he grew up and which was the setting for his dream-adventure. It is many years since he visited the house, which now belongs to his brother, George. He finds there a story he had written as a child which describes the dream but which, in Wilditch's eyes, 'falsifies' and 'betrays' its 'integrity'. He therefore decides to write a second, honest account of the experience, and this constitutes the Second Part of the story.

While exploring an island in a lake at the bottom of the garden, the young Wilditch had discovered a hidden passageway which led deep into the earth. Entering the tunnel, he met Javitt, an incredibly ancient misanthrope living underground with Maria, an equally strange woman. Javitt had a hoard of old newspapers at least fifty years out of date, and a secret treasure which he showed Wilditch. The boy is also deeply impressed by Javitt's rather offbeat philsophy of life:

'Be disloyal. It's your duty to the human race. The human race needs to survive and it's the loyal man who dies first from anxiety or a bullet or overwork. If you have to earn a living, boy, and the price they make you pay is loyalty, be a double agent – and never let either of the two sides know your real name. The same applies to women and God. They both respect a man they don't own . . .'

Javitt also claimed that a girl pictured in one of the newspapers as the winner of the Miss Ramsgate beauty contest was his daughter. Wilditch fell in love with her and decided to dedicate his life to finding her. Javitt warned him that he would have to travel every continent in his search, though he could sensibly 'leave out the Arctic and the North Pole – she was always a warm girl':

And it occurs to me now when I think of the life I have led since, that I have been in most of those regions . . . It was as though the purpose of life had suddenly come to me . . .

'Under the Garden' differs from the studies of childhood conditioning we have seen in the other stories because Wilditch's fate, or what Greene calls his 'future', is seen as part of his character, and therefore as something he cannot avoid – rather than as something imposed on him by the external course of events as in 'The Basement Room'. Thus, although the search for Javitt's daughter gives his endless travels 'a purpose', he was already a restless traveller full of 'curiosity' before he met Javitt:

'All the rough journeys of the future were already in me then, like a muscle which only had to develop.'

Similarly, although Wilditch learns more about life from Javitt 'than from all my schoolmasters', he reminds us in the same sentence that this influence comes from a 'man who never existed' – in other words, from his own imagination.

Despite writing down all he can remember of Javitt, the adult Wilditch remains unable to decide whether this formative experience actually happened, or whether it was in fact a dream, and at the end the reader is also left in doubt as to what is fact and what is fantasy. Wilditch re-explores the island, looking for the entrance to Javitt's cave, and finds the 'golden po' Javitt had given to him as a souvenir. However, what in his dream was a great treasure, turns out to be a battered tin chamber-pot, to which adhered 'a few flakes of yellow paint':

Had he then really dropped this in his flight – which meant that somewhere underneath him now Javitt sat on his lavatory seat and Maria quacked beside the calor-gas . . .? There was no certainty; perhaps years ago, when the paint was fresh, he had discovered the pot, just as he had done this day, and founded a whole afternoon-legend around it.

Part of the relationship between imagination and reality in the story is the connection between art and life. Wilditch's dream (if it is a dream) has a very literary flavour to it, and is obviously determined by the books he had been reading as a child – *Treasure Island, Coral Island, Robinson Crusoe* and *The Romance of Australian Exploration*. As in a boy's adventure story, he gives names to the stages of his underground journey: Friday's Cave, Camp Indecision and Camp Hope. However, it is not just Wilditch's dream which has been conditioned by the books he has read. His whole life, we are told, had been formed 'not by Javitt, but by Grey and Burke' (characters in *The Romance of Australian Exploration*).

On one level 'Under the Garden' is also about the act of writing itself, and about the writer's responsibilities to truth. Wilditch writes two accounts of his underground experience. In the story he wrote as a child (signed W.W.) the real experience is 'falsified' into a stock schoolboy adventure, a conventionalized fantasy devoid of any personal meaning. In the second account, written at the end of his life, he tries to get to the heart of the matter, and is intent not only on telling the truth, but on understanding its significance. As he does so he begins to realize that W.W. had been 'afraid' to acknowledge the true meaning of the dream-adventure. His mother had feared that his story of an underground search for hidden treasure was a symbolic expression of a religious 'curiosity', and he had therefore tried to disguise it, like a secret agent who uses a cover story to deceive his interrogators. Now his mother is dead and 'beyond hurt', however, Wilditch is free to tell the truth and able at last to understand the true nature of his experience: 'Across the pond the bell rang for breakfast and he thought, "Poor mother – she had reason to fear", turning the tin chamber-pot on his lap.'

The chamber-pot is a potent image in the story. On the one hand, as part of the religious theme it can be taken as a parody of the Holy Grail. On the other hand it represents the transformation of experience into art in the hands of the novelist. However, the novelist is not an alchemist and cannot change base metal into gold, as W.W. had tried to do. He has a responsibility to the truth of experience and should not pretend that a painted tin chamber-pot is a fabulous 'golden po'.

4 Saved by Disloyalty

I

Brighton Rock is the first of Greene's so-called Catholic novels –
the first of his novels to have a conscious and strongly defined
'religious sense'. In an essay on François Mauriac Greene stated
his belief that with the death of Henry James the religious sense
was lost to the English novel. This was a 'disaster', for 'with the
religious sense went the sense of the importance of the human
act. It was as if the world of fiction had lost a dimension: the
characters of such distinguished writers as Mrs Virginia Woolf
and Mr E. M. Forster wandered like cardboard symbols through
a world that was paper thin'. In 'traditional' novels, on the other
hand, 'characters have the solidity and importance of men with
souls to save or lose'. In *Brighton Rock* Greene made an attempt
to restore this religious sense to the novel. In doing so, he makes
his criminal characters risk not only arrest and imprisonment, as
in the usual thriller, but also eternal damnation. The stakes are
raised, and Greene exploits the dramatic advantage this offers.

Brighton Rock is the story of Pinkie, a young and ruthless
member of the Brighton underworld who has assumed leadership
of a small-time gang working a protection racket, after its former
leader, Kite, is killed by Raven (the hero of *A Gun for Sale*).
Pinkie murders a pathetic journalist called Hale, who has double-
crossed the gang, but although the police fail to solve the crime,
Ida, a casual acquaintance of Hale's, is determined to seek
'justice' on his behalf. Her relentless pursuit of Pinkie drives him
to murder others, including Spicer, a member of the gang, and to
marry an innocent young waitress, Rose, to prevent her giving
evidence in court against him. Later, however, when he tries to
trick Rose into committing suicide by a fake 'pact', he is
interrupted by Ida and the police and in the resulting struggle he

accidentally splashes his own eyes with the vitriol he always carries with him, and in agony falls over the cliff edge to his death. Both Pinkie and Rose are Roman Catholics and their faith strongly colours their view of life. Pinkie's corruption and Rose's innocence meet in a curious way through their faith, as we shall see later. They are contrasted to simple, vigorous, fun-loving Ida, who represents 'common decency' but whose lack of religion makes her somehow less of a person than even the evil Pinkie, and much has been made of Greene's lack of sympathy for her.

In his portrait of Pinkie Greene was trying, 'as a sort of intellectual exercise', he tells us in *The Other Man*, to create a character one could credibly imagine as being damned by God for his actions. Evelyn Waugh, reviewing the novel in *The Tablet*, found Pinkie to be 'completely damnable . . . the ideal examinee for entry to Hell, who gets a pure alpha on every paper'. However, in the words of Unamuno, 'doing evil is not the same as being evil', and despite the pure malice of Pinkie's actions and intentions Waugh is clearly wrong, for the novel makes a strong case in Pinkie's defence.

Like Raven's in *A Gun for Sale*, Pinkie's social background is one of misery and deprivation and this is largely responsible for his later delinquency. Greene himself admits in *The Other Man* that Pinkie is not guilty of mortal sin 'because his actions were not committed in defiance of God, but arose out of the conditions to which he had been born'. He had even thought of being a priest until the bitterness of experience, and the subsequent kindness shown to him by his father-figure, Kite, drew him into the ranks of the lawless.

Pinkie's sins, then, are not, as Waugh claims, the expression of an inherent evil. His acts of violent sadism, for example, his pinching of Rose's wrist until she cries, his desire to tear the sticking plaster from Spicer's wound 'and see the skin break', are a reaction to, and revenge for, his own sufferings. Pinkie is an alienated figure, at war with society and incapable of any close relationship. Like the boy Philip in 'The Basement Room', he has 'extricated himself from life'. He has a 'sick horror' of sex which he avoids with 'a kind of hideous and unnatural pride': his 'soured virginity' is a sign of his refusal to become involved with life, as is his puritanical refusal to smoke or drink.

He does become 'involved', however, despite himself, when he finds himself forced to marry Rose to prevent her giving evidence against him. Marriage, intimate attachment to another human being, is like 'ordure on the hands' for Pinkie, while the fact that they are not 'properly married' (that is, by a priest), and therefore guilty of fornication, is for him the final step towards inevitable damnation. As it turns out, however, the sexual act awakens in him a sort of love:

It seemed to him more like death than when Hale and Spicer had died . . . He had an odd sense of triumph: he had graduated in the last human shame – it wasn't so difficult after all . . . He didn't need Mr Prewitt or Spicer, only – a faint feeling of tenderness woke for his partner in the act.

Later, as Pinkie is putting into operation his plan for Rose's murder, driving towards the lonely cliff edge and to what Rose understands to be a suicide pact, he thinks: 'He hadn't hated her; he hadn't even hated the act. There had been a kind of pleasure, a kind of pride, a kind of – something else.' There is a suggestion here of a connection between profane and sacred forms of love, a suggestion that Pinkie could find redemption through human love, even through sex itself. This idea was to become a central theme of *The End of the Affair*, though Greene does not develop it further here.

Pinkie and Rose's drive through the rain, pursued by Ida and the police, is the climax of the story, the moment of the most intense excitement and tension, and it is here that Pinkie experiences the direct presence of God in his life. As with the whisky priest's vision of God's love in *The Power and the Glory*, religious experience for Pinkie assumes a nightmarish form:

An enormous emotion beat on him; it was like something trying to get in; the pressure of gigantic wings against the glass. Dona nobis pacem. He withstood it . . . If the glass broke, if the beast – whatever it was – got in, God knows what it would do. He had a sense of huge havoc – the confession, the penance and the sacrament – and awful distraction, and he drove blind into the rain.

Pinkie is pursued ruthlessly both by God and by the secular forces of Ida and the police, just as the whisky priest is pursued by God and the police lieutenant. God tries to force his way through Pinkie's resistance by 'breaking' the glass and ironically three pages later the image is picked up: 'Glass – somewhere – broke.' This, however, is the glass bottle of vitriol which splashes in his face and sends him, in agony, over the cliff. The ending is deliberately ambiguous. Did he fall or did he throw himself? Did he find, as he had hoped, God's mercy 'between the stirrup and the ground', pardoning him for his sins? We are told that as he fell it was 'as if he'd been withdrawn suddenly by a hand out of any existence', and if this is the hand of God there is no suggestion of divine forgiveness, or of God bringing Pinkie into His presence, for the hand has 'whipped' him away 'into zero – nothing'. However, we are warned against drawing any conclusions about Pinkie's supernatural fate by the priest. He tells Rose: ' "You can't conceive, my child, nor can I or anyone the . . . appalling . . . strangeness of the mercy of God".'

This phrase sums up the novel's preoccupation with the mystery of divine justice. Greene was at the time strongly influenced by the powerful, nonconformist writings of the French poet and essayist Charles Péguy. In one of his essays, 'Saints and Sinners', which has been quoted on several occasions by Greene, Péguy states:

The sinner lies at the very heart of Christianity . . . The sinner and the saint are, one can say, two portions equally integral, two equally integral parts of the Christian mechanism.

I noted earlier how Pinkie's corruption and Rose's innocence are closely interconnected in the novel, exactly in the manner described by Péguy. They 'belong together', like Péguy's saint and sinner, they are 'the two sides of the same coin'. The influence of Péguy on Greene's thinking in the matter is underlined by the priest at the end. Rose has decided that if Pinkie has been damned for his sins – as she believes – then she will be damned with him. She even regrets not having killed herself as Pinkie had wanted her to. The priest then talks to her of love, and to her surprise tells her the story of Péguy's taking sides with the damned against God's justice. He even compares her to Péguy (though he never mentions his name):

'There was a man, a Frenchman, you wouldn't know about him, my child, who had the same idea as you. He was a good man, a holy man, and he lived in sin all through his life, because he couldn't bear the idea that any soul could suffer damnation.' She listened with astonishment. He said, 'This man decided that if any soul was going to be damned, he would be damned too. He never took the sacraments, he never married his wife in church. I don't know my child, but some people think he was – well, a saint. I think he died in what we are told is mortal sin – I'm not sure: it was in the war: perhaps . . . It was a case of greater love hath no man than this that he lay down his soul for his friend.'

The priest's message here is one that we meet in all of Greene's writings, the belief that in the end it is on love that we will be judged.

Also in 'Saints and Sinners', Péguy wrote that 'a man who is not a Christian is a man who does not sin.' He likened Christianity to a city: 'A bad citizen belongs to the city. A good stranger does not.' This suggests that it is better spiritually, if not morally, to be a sinful Christian than to be a good atheist, and this conflict is taken up by Greene in his characterizations of Pinkie and Ida. What has antagonized many readers is the fact that in the novel Pinkie, despite his evil, is seen as close to God and even pursued by God, whereas the 'good' Ida is 'as far from them [Pinkie and Rose] as she [is] from Hell – or Heaven'. Ida is an example of common human decency. We are told repeatedly that she knows right from wrong – words which, on the other hand, mean nothing to Rose: '. . . their taste was extinguished by stronger foods – Good and Evil.'

One of the adjectives most frequently used to describe Pinkie is 'sick', while Ida is 'healthy', or 'normal'. She is part of the great mass of holidaymakers on Brighton front, enjoying life and out for a good time, though with a strong moral code. But this moral code appears to stand for nothing. Ida lacks a religious dimension and therefore lacks importance. Her actions do not have the supernatural importance of Pinkie's.

This paradox at the heart of *Brighton Rock* is summed up in another essay of importance to Greene at this time, T. S. Eliot's 'Baudelaire':

So far as we are human, what we do must be either evil or good; so far as we do evil or good we are human; and it is better, in a paradoxical way, to do evil, than to do nothing: at least we exist. It is true to say that the glory of man is his capacity for salvation; it is also true to say that his glory is his capacity for damnation. The worst that can be said for most of our malefactors, from statesmen to thieves, is that they are not men enough to be damned.

However, in Eliot's terms Pinkie is also, like Ida, not 'man enough to be damned', simply because he is a victim, a product of social conditioning and therefore not truly responsible for his actions. Indeed, it would seem that Greene's God, as we meet Him in the novels, is not God enough to damn anyone anyway. God is omniscient, therefore there must be extenuating circumstances for everyone's evil; everyone must be a 'special case'. He explains in *The Other Man*:

God's justice derives from total knowledge. This is the reason why I don't believe in hell: if God exists – I'm not convinced He does – He is omniscient; if He is omniscient, I can't bring myself to imagine that a creature conceived by Him can be so evil as to merit eternal punishment. His grace must intervene at some point.

Greene began writing *Brighton Rock* as an 'entertainment', a straight thriller about gang warfare and protection rackets in contemporary Brighton, and it was only after he had begun it that Pinkie's religious beliefs assumed an overriding importance in the novel's thematic scheme. It is perhaps for this reason – that it was not planned as a 'religious novel' – that the religious theme appears imposed on the novel rather than being an integral part of the artistic whole. The religious scruples of Greene's gangsters lack credibility, and this leads to incongruities in their characters. For example, most critics find Pinkie's famous parody of the opening of the Apostles' Creed ('*Credo in unum Satunum*') to be beyond his limited intellectual powers, while Rose's saintliness and her Péguy-like self-damnation seem due more to simple-mindedness than to any inherent goodness or innocence.

Brighton Rock nevertheless remains one of Greene's triumphs, particularly in its dynamic use of language which is poetic in its intensity and sensory vividness. Pinkie's abnormal attitude to sex, for example, is expressed in terms of sickness and poison:

He watched her with his soured virginity, as one might watch a draught of medicine offered that one would never, never take; one would die first – or let others die.

Elsewhere we are told that 'there was poison in his veins, though he grinned and bore it'; and that the poison 'twists in the Boy's veins'. K. W. Gransden, in his essay on Greene's rhetoric, has mentioned also the 'strange, nightmarish animal imagery' that pervades the novel, for example when the dead Spicer lies at the bottom of the stairs, the rotten wood lies across his body in the sinister form of 'a walnut-stained eagle crouched over the kidneys'.

The emptiness of Ida's carefree, healthy world is also suggested through imagery. She is continually presented as a mother-figure, to Hale and especially to Rose, whose actual mother she pretends to be. However, her 'big breasts . . . had never suckled a child of her own'. This, in a mother-figure, is a wilful sterility which when contrasted to Rose's fertility (she is pregnant at the end of the novel) would seem to have spiritual undertones. Sex for Ida is purely pleasure, like life. The 'reward' of life for her, however, is described almost in terms of disgust: '. . . the soft gluey mouth affixed in taxis, the warm handclasp in cinemas, the only reward there was'.

All Ida's worldly 'rewards' end in emptiness or disillusion. In sex, 'men always failed you when it came to the act: she might just as well have been to the pictures'. She is part of the holiday crowd in the 'bright glittering Brighton air', but again the language reveals a sense of corruption and emptiness within the crowd 'as it uncoiled endlessly . . . like a twisted piece of wire, two by two, each with an air of sober and determined gaiety'. This is not true happiness, but people distracting themselves from their misery with Guinness and oysters and the cheap amusements of the pier.

The view of life expressed in *Brighton Rock* is bleak and pessimistic, and nowhere more so than in those moments of savagely ironical humour which are scattered throughout the novel. After Hale's death Ida attends his cremation in London: 'Fred dropped in indistinguishable ash on the pink blossoms: he became part of the smoke nuisance over London, and Ida wept.'

Later, Pinkie recalls the story of Annie Collins (a true story which Greene also recounts in *The Lawless Roads*):

'She put her head on the line,' he said, 'up by the Hassocks. She had to wait ten minutes for the seven-five. Fog made it late from Victoria. Cut off her head. She was fifteen. She was going to have a baby and she knew what it was like. She'd had one two years before, and they could 'ave pinned it on twelve boys.'

It is the gruesome yet laughable detail of the delayed train, the exposure of the banal at the heart of human tragedy, which is characteristic of Greene's particular form of pessimism.

It is significant also that in the factual account of the same story given in *The Lawless Roads*, the girl's boyfriend commits suicide with her, and that Greene chooses to omit this detail in the fictional version. He does not like to dilute the misery of his characters and indeed some critics have accused him of 'turning the knife in the wound'. Such is the case at the end of *Brighton Rock*, when Rose leaves the priest to go home and listen to the message Pinkie had recorded on their wedding day. Then she 'walked rapidly in the thin June sunlight towards the worst horror of all', the discovery of what the reader has known all along to have been a message, not of tenderness and affection, but of a blind and evil hatred.

II

In *Brighton Rock* the struggle between secular and religious values takes place against a violent background. However, on Greene's visit to Mexico in 1938 to research a report commissioned by the Catholic Church on religious persecution under the new revolutionary socialist regime, he discovered a situation in which this struggle had literally become a matter of life and death. The experience of Mexico affected Greene profoundly. It was this, combined with 'General Franco's attack on Republican Spain', which 'inextricably involved religion in contemporary life' for him:

I think it was under those two influences – and the backward and forward sway of my sympathies – that I began to examine more closely the effect of faith on action. Catholicism was no longer primarily symbolic, a ceremony at an altar with the correct canonical number of candles, with the women in my Chelsea congregation wearing their best hats, nor was it a philosophical page in Father D'Arcy's *Nature of Belief.* It was closer now to death in the afternoon.

(*WE*)

The dramatic intensity of the Mexican situation was soon translated into fiction by Greene, resulting in one of his finest achievements. The main character of *The Power and the Glory* is an unnamed 'whisky priest' who is pursued, like Pinkie, by the police on the one hand and by his conscience and his God on the other. He is the last active priest in the province, defying the government ban against saying Mass. He lives as a fugitive, but the villagers among whom he hides are torn between their natural desire to harbour and protect him and their fear of retribution from the police. In the event many lose their lives because of him. The priest is pursued, and finally captured, by an idealistic socialist police lieutenant (also unnamed) who is a fanatical atheist and anti-clerical. The priest is executed, and although in the eyes of the official Church he was a sinner, a drunken coward who had been unable to keep the rules of his faith and who even had a bastard child from one of his peasant parishioners, the conclusion is that he is a good, and even holy, man. The novel ends with a new, also unnamed, priest appearing in the town after the execution to continue the work of the dead whisky priest.

As a religious novel, *The Power and the Glory* works far better than *Brighton Rock*: the religious theme is integrated into the story rather than being imposed on it. Among the race-track gangs and holidaymakers in Brighton, theological debate seemed out of place, but it is not out of character in a priest nor strange in a society enduring religious persecution. The novel's success in this respect is perhaps also due to the simplicity of the plot which, while full of danger and suspense on an 'entertaining' level, is well able to support its allegorical implications. Although a journey is a standard metaphor for spiritual self-discovery,

Greene creates something original here by turning the chase of modern melodramatic fiction into a metaphor for spiritual experience. Thanks to his long apprenticeship in the earlier entertainments, Greene transforms religious debate in *The Power and the Glory* into a tense, exciting and colourful drama, as gripping as it is thought-provoking.

One of the main points of Greene's thesis in the novel is that in a priest the man is separate from his office, so that despite being corrupt – perhaps even damned – he can still put God into the mouths of men. This 'separateness' is not true of the 'religion' of socialism, however. On the contrary, the purely secular ideals of the party are founded entirely on man's capacity for good, and can thus be irreparably damaged by the weakness or corruption of individuals (the simple technique of withholding the names of both protagonists and referring to them only by their titles of office emphasizes this). The priest makes the same point himself during his political argument with the police lieutenant, after his arrest:

'That's another difference between us. It's no good your working for your end unless you're a good man yourself. And there won't always be good men in your party. Then you'll have all the old starvation, beating, get-rich-anyhow. But it doesn't matter so much my being a coward – and all the rest. I can put God into a man's mouth just the same – and I can give him God's pardon. It wouldn't make any difference to that if every priest in the Church was like me.'

In 'Why Do I Write?' (1948) Greene stated his belief that a novelist's integrity depended on his 'disloyalty'. In political terms, this meant that it was a writer's duty to be 'a piece of grit in the machinery of state'. In moral terms, it meant being 'allowed to write from the point of view of the black square as well as the white'. Indeed, he went on to say that although he was a member of the Catholic Church, as an artist he was 'saved by [his] disloyalty' to that Church, for if all that he wrote of Catholicism conformed with official dogma, the result would be propaganda. In *The Power and the Glory* this disloyalty is evident in Greene's decision to portray the priest as corrupt, and the police lieutenant, the atheist man of violence, as incorruptible. The comparison between the two is emphasized by many references to the lieutenant's ideological and moral purity, which are couched in quasi-religious terms: 'There was something of a priest in his intent, observant walk – a theologian going back over the errors of the past to destroy them again.' The lieutenant's fanatical dedication to social-ism, his atheistic 'certainty', is described as a form of mysticism:

There are mystics who are said to have experienced God directly. He was a mystic, too, and what he had experienced was vacancy – a complete certainty in the existence of a dying, cooling world, of human beings who had evolved from animals for no purpose at all. He knew.

The lieutenant's compassion for the poor is contrasted to the heartless and uncharitable piety of several of the religious characters, particularly the pious woman the priest meets in the prison cell and the pious mother of the boy Luis. These women are as comfortable and shallow in their belief as Ida was in her unbelief. Like her, the women claim to know what God does or does not 'mind' (though the priest, who is seen at the end to be truly holy, humbly admits he does not 'know a thing about the mercy of God', he does not know 'how awful the human heart looks to Him'). François Mauriac in *Men I Hold Great* saw the novel as 'a great lesson' to those, like Luis's mother, who are 'obsessed with perfection':

. . . those scrupulous people who split hairs over their shortcomings, and who forget that, in the last day, according to the word of St John of the Cross, it is on love that they will be judged.

The spiritual progress of the priest from a similarly heartless piety (as a young priest in an affluent parish he had been as comfortable and complacent as any) towards love, reaches its climax at the moment of his greatest degradation: the first night he spends in the prison cell, having been arrested for drinking alcohol forbidden under the new prohibition laws. This is the central scene in the book and one of the most effective passages Greene has ever written. The priest, who is disguised as a peasant, is thrown into a common cell with criminals and prostitutes, who urinate and fornicate in the darkness around him. It is in this setting that the priest finally loses his pride and learns instead the power of love and humility:

What an unbearable creature he must have been in those days – and yet in those days he had been comparatively innocent. That was another mystery: it sometimes seemed to him that venial sins – impatience, an unimportant lie, pride, a neglected opportunity – cut you off from grace more completely than the worst sins of all. Then, in his innocence, he had felt no love for anyone; now in his corruption he had learnt . . .

We are back here in the paradoxical world of Péguy: the sinner is at the very heart of Christianity and closest to the sinner is the saint, and indeed here they are one and the same person. In his youth the priest had been without sin, but also without love. Later, when he is full of sin and apparently totally corrupted, his capacity for love overrides all.

The paradoxical saintliness of the priest is effectively underlined by a direct and ironical comparison with the life of another fictional saint, Juan, read aloud to Luis by his devout mother. This repellent 'book within a book' is, in its smug, assured sense of holiness and spiritual self-satisfaction, a subtle and accomplished parody of much Church propaganda:

Did any premonition touch young Juan that night that he, too, in a few short years, would be numbered among the martyrs? We cannot say, but Father Miguel Cerra tells how that evening Juan spent longer than usual upon his knees, and when his class-mates teased him a little, as boys will . . .

Unlike young Juan, however, the whisky priest has an uneasy relationship with his God, who pursues him with even greater determination than does the law. The priest views God's love with a mixture of awe and fear:

It set fire to a bush in the desert, didn't it, and smashed open graves and set the dead walking in the dark. Oh, a man like me would run a mile to get away if he felt that love around.

The priest comes closest to a dialogue with God when he is taken back to the prison to await execution. It is then that he attempts to strike a Péguy-like bargain with God, offering his soul for damnation if the soul of his illegitimate daughter Brigitta, who even as a child is seen to be corrupt and sinful, can be saved:

'Damn me, I deserve it, but let her live for ever.' This bargain is seen as a measure of the priest's power of love, for it is the same intense love described by the priest in *Brighton Rock* as 'greater love hath no man than this that he lay down his soul for his friend'. It is also a measure of the priest's humility, for he learns that he is incapable of loving all mankind, as God has instructed us to, but can only love his own child: 'This was the love he should have felt for every soul in the world.'

The fact that Brigitta is corrupt and unlovable strengthens the religious analogy here. If his child had been the planter's daughter, Coral, who sheltered the priest from the police, his emotional attachment to her would have been easily understood. But the priest loves Brigitta simply because she is his own creation and, though it is not directly stated, the reader cannot miss the implication that if the priest can create something which is corrupt yet love it notwithstanding, then God can love his creation too despite its inherent corruption.

The novel is full of children, who play an important role in the story. This is particularly true of the boy Luis, who admires the police lieutenant and hates the pious propaganda stories read to him by his mother. However, after witnessing the martyrdom of the whisky priest (whom his mother despises) Luis changes his allegiance and it is he who at the end of the novel welcomes the new fugitive priest into the house – the priest who will carry on the solitary and illegal ministry. Just before his death, the whisky priest feels 'an immense disappointment because he had to go to God empty-handed, with nothing done at all'. However, it is Luis's conversion, unknown to him, which suggests that this is not in fact the case, that despite his miserable example of sinfulness as a priest he has touched the hearts of people and brought them to God.

In *The Power and the Glory* Greene takes the first step towards combining religion and politics into a single theme, a combination which was to give such strength to his later novels. The atheistic police lieutenant is fighting an idealistic crusade to liberate the oppressed by eradicating social injustice and with it 'the Church which not only preaches passive acceptance of this injustice but supports it'. Instead of prayers and hope of a better life after death, he intends to give the poor food and the power of literacy.

It is significant that the despised holier-than-thou Catholics in the novel are all educated and well-off. Greene, on the other hand, seems to admire the simple faith of the poor and in particular the powerful emblems of the Indians' primitive religion, the crosses which were 'like trees that had been left to seed', and which seem 'like a short cut to the dark and magical heart of the faith'. The whisky priest himself abandons the rich and pious of his early parish for the poor peasants, and his message of hope to the poor is curious in that it echoes the lieutenant's own secular ideals of creating heaven here on earth by defining heaven in purely social and political terms: ' "Heaven is where there is no *jefe*, no unjust laws, no taxes, no soldiers and no hunger . . . There are no Red Shirts. Nobody grows old. The crops never fail." '

Although siding emotionally with the poor, the priest is ideologically opposed to the idea of revolution. We have already seen his distrust of political systems due to their reliance on human nature. In his discussion with the lieutenant he goes further and suggests that poverty is a form of innocence and that the poor should not be corrupted by being made rich:

'We've already said the poor are blessed and the rich are going to find it hard to get into heaven. Why should we make it hard for the poor man too? Oh, I know we are told to give to the poor, to see that they are not hungry – hunger can make a man do evil just as much as money can. But why should we give the poor power? It's better to let him die in dirt and wake in heaven – so long as we don't push his face in the dirt.'

In *The Lawless Roads* Greene had written of the Catholic Church in Mexico under the oppression, that it had to 'relearn the technique of revolution'. This, since 1940, is exactly what it has done throughout Latin America with the emergence there of Liberation Theology. As we shall see later, this is a movement which has particular attractions for Greene and in the later novels, from *The Comedians* on, far from distrusting revolution, Greene's priests assume leading roles in politics and actively participate in helping the oppressed in their struggle for political liberation.

5 A Village Struck with Plague

Jean-Paul Sartre once accused François Mauriac of playing God
in his novels, and though this is true of Greene only in so much as
it is true of any other realist novelist who has total control over
the fate of his characters, one could accuse many of Greene's
critics of playing St Peter, deciding which characters to let
through the gates of heaven and which to send down to hell. *The
Heart of the Matter*, in particular, has been used as the text for a
debate which belongs more to the realms of moral theology and
eschatology than of literature, despite Greene's repeated insis-
tence that the book is fiction, not renegade theology; that the
existence of a Catholic literature is 'impossible'; and that it is the
'human factor' that interests him, 'not apologetics'.

That said, however, *The Heart of the Matter* is above all about
religion. Catholicism is the frame of reference by which the
characters, and their author, interpret the events described, and
so any discussion of the book must concentrate on this theme.

Scobie, a Catholic English policeman in a godforsaken back-
water of colonial West Africa, is yet again passed over for
promotion. This brings the social and emotional frustrations of
his hysterical and depressed wife to crisis point, so that she
appears to be on the verge of a nervous breakdown. Louise is a
pious and unlikeable woman whom Scobie has long ceased to
love, though he pities her and feels protective towards her, and in
order to send her on a much needed holiday he borrows money
from Yusef, a corrupt Syrian merchant. While Louise is away,
Scobie falls in love with Helen, a pathetic child widow, though
again love is confused with pity in Scobie's heart and he becomes
incapable of reconciling the emotional demands made on him by

both women, as well as incapable of reconciling his infidelity with his conscience. Scobie assumes the responsibility for the happiness of both Louise and Helen and his inability to hurt either of them involves him in lies and deceptions, which lead inexorably to his own death as he sees suicide as the only way out of a situation in which his very existence is a source of pain to those he cares for.

Like Rose and the whisky priest (and Péguy), Scobie deliberately chooses to damn himself out of love for others (despair, according to the teaching of the Catholic Church, is the 'unforgivable sin'). Again, however, Greene questions the traditional concept of divine punishment as well as the role of the Church as an intermediary between man and his creator, and the Church's moral authority is seen in the novel as undermined by the overriding and anarchic power of love.

In *A Sort of Life* Greene describes how in 1928, as a recent convert to Catholicism, he consulted a priest about a personal moral dilemma: he was about to be married but had suddenly been led to believe that he was epileptic, and if this were indeed the case, he intended to avoid having children. The priest warned, however, that under no circumstances was contraception permissible and that the Church expected him, in such a predicament, to marry and 'trust God'. This rigidity horrified Greene, but it also impressed him: 'It was the Rock of Peter I was aware of in our long drive, and though it repulsed me, I couldn't help admiring its unyielding façade.'

Since then the Catholic Church has changed considerably with emphasis placed on individual conscience rather than hard-and-fast rules. However, it was under the *ancien régime* that Greene entered the Church, in the days before the Second Vatican Council. Then 'there was only one hard answer' a priest could give in any situation, despite his own compassion and understanding, and that was an answer in accordance with the law as laid down by the Church – which 'knows all the rules', as Father Rank, Scobie's priest, says in *The Heart of the Matter*.

In his Catholic novels Greene explores situations which reveal the conflict between the rigidity of the Church's rules and, again in Father Rank's words, 'what goes on in a . . . human heart'. About this the Church 'knows nothing', and in its response to human problems in the novels the Church is almost invariably seen as inadequate. It is also seen as being without any infallible authority in eschatological matters or in interpreting God's love and mercy, to quote Father Rank again: 'For goodness' sake, Mrs Scobie, don't think you – or I – know a thing about God's mercy'. In particular, Greene questions text-book moral theology which, in Unamuno's words, has turned religion 'into a kind of police system', and in many of the novels there is a defiance of this authority. Everyone is seen to be 'a special case' (the Church's own argument against *The Power and the Glory*, which it placed on its index of prohibited books) and characters who come closest to a final state of grace are those who have broken the Church's rules: the whisky priest in *The Power and the Glory*, Sarah in *The End of the Affair*, Father Rivas in *The Honorary Consul* and Scobie in *The Heart of the Matter*.

Its moral and dogmatic paradoxes make *The Heart of the Matter* Greene's most problematic novel and make Scobie the character critics disagree about most. Greene's initial intention was to develop the theme of pity which he had already treated in his last book, *The Ministry of Fear*, to show how it can be 'the expression of an almost monstrous pride'. But, as he wrote in *Ways of Escape*, the effect on readers was quite different: '. . . to them Scobie was exonerated, Scobie was "a good man", he was hunted to his doom by the harshness of his wife.'

Scobie is undoubtedly a good man, an honest man who is corrupted not by money or power but by sentiment and a sense of responsibility for the happiness of others, which leads him to the extreme of wishing to damn himself not so that others will be saved, in the manner of the whisky priest and of Charles Péguy, but so that they shall not suffer in this world. Like Rowe in *The Ministry of Fear*, he cannot bear the sight of another's pain, but his predicament is worse than Rowe's because he himself is the instrument that causes the pain, having become trapped in an emotional dilemma which can only be solved by betraying and therefore hurting either Louise, his wife, or Helen, his lover.

Scobie's sense of pity leads him not only to despair but to conscious blasphemy in his note sparing Helen from pain, saying that he loves her more than he loves God, and in protecting Louise from the truth by going to communion with her even though he is in a state of mortal sin. Both these acts are instances of how religion is carefully integrated into the plot. The blasphemous note, the first sign of Scobie's spiritual corruption, becomes the instrument of his actual corruption when it is intercepted by Yusef, who uses it to blackmail Scobie into breaking the law. The communion shows not only Scobie's weakness but also Louise's ruthlessness, for ironically she knows of her husband's adultery, and uses the sacrament as a weapon: either he will confess his sin to the priest and give up his affair, or he will be forced to make an open declaration of it. In the event, however, he does neither, and Louise is shown to have underestimated the limits to which his sense of pity will take him.

God enters the story almost as a character and becomes in turn a victim of Scobie's pity, for Scobie's final decision to kill himself is as much due to wishing to spare God (who is 'ill with me', whose 'punch-drunk head' is 'reeling sideways') further suffering, as to spare Louise and Helen further unhappiness. Scobie's sense of pity and responsibility leads to a spiritual egotism which is a form of pride, as well as to despair, as he is not only his brother's keeper but pretends to be his God's keeper as well. The moral paradox here, however, is twofold. Firstly, if God created him, then He must share the blame for the way Scobie is: 'If you made me, you made this feeling of responsibility that I've always carried about like a sack of bricks.' Secondly, his act of despair is also an act of atonement, an act born not out of a sense of evil or hatred of God, but out of a sense of goodness and love of God:

Despair is the price one pays for setting oneself an impossible aim. It is, one is told, the unforgivable sin, but it is a sin the corrupt or evil man never practises . . . Only the man of goodwill carries always in his heart this capacity for damnation.

Scobie takes this strongly deterministic and pessimistic view of life even further, to the point of implicating Christ in His own betrayal and suggesting that He too committed suicide, for if God exists then He must be all-powerful, and man's sin must be an integral part of His plan:

God had sometimes broken his own laws and was it less possible for him to put out a hand of forgiveness into the suicidal darkness than

to have woken himself in the tomb, behind the stone? Christ had not
been murdered: you couldn't murder God. Christ had killed himself: he
had hung himself on the Cross as surely as Pemberton from the picture
rail.

These are clues that Scobie is in two minds, as is his creator
(and Greene boldly exercises here what he considers his right to
comment on his characters) about whether God will damn him.
Scobie cannot believe in a God 'who was not human enough to
love what he had created', and later he tells Helen that 'against
all the teaching of the Church, one has the conviction that love –
any kind of love – does deserve a bit of mercy.' Although 'one
will pay terribly', he does not believe that 'one will pay for ever'.
Here again, love is the agent of grace and redemption and it is
surely significant that Scobie dies with the word 'love' on his lips.
However, as in *Brighton Rock*, a priest appears to warn against
drawing conclusions, for man's eternal destiny is decided by 'the
appalling strangeness of the mercy of God', which is beyond the
capacity of man himself to know or comprehend:

'For goodness' sake, Mrs. Scobie, don't imagine you – or I – know a
thing about God's mercy.'
'The Church says . . .'
'I know the Church says. The Church knows all the rules. But it
doesn't know what goes on in a single human heart.'
'You think there's some hope then?' she wearily asked.
'Are you so bitter against him?'
'I haven't any bitterness left.'
'And do you think God's likely to be more bitter than a woman?'

Of all Greene's characters, Scobie is perhaps the most difficult
for a non-Catholic to sympathize with. His unwavering acceptance
of the Church's teachings, and in particular of the doctrine of
eternal punishment in which he has a rather over-scrupulous
belief, has in turn to be accepted by the reader if Scobie is to
come alive. Greene himself finds Scobie's religious scruples 'too
extreme', and one of the most devastating critiques of the book
came from George Orwell, who thought the theological nature of
Scobie's dilemma 'snobbish' and 'sinister'. In his essay 'The Sanc-
tified Sinner' he holds him up to ridicule:

White all through, with a stiff upper lip, he had gone to what he believed
to be certain damnation out of pure gentlemanliness . . .

If he believed in Hell, he would not risk going there merely to spare the
feelings of a couple of neurotic women.

Although Greene portrays Scobie's dilemma in a sympathetic
and compassionate light, Scobie's lack of self-understanding is
exaggerated, his religious conscience over-scrupulous and his
self-judgment too pitiless, particularly for one so consumed with
pity for others and professing a belief in God's love and mercy.
As Orwell points out, 'trying to clothe theological speculations in
flesh and blood . . . produces psychological absurdities', such as
that a man whose chief characteristic is a horror of causing pain
'would not be an officer in a colonial police force' (Orwell is
speaking from personal experience). The result is that what was
intended as a personal and spiritual tragedy degenerates into a
theological melodrama.

Orwell also criticized the African setting of the novel which
was, he claimed, superfluous: 'Except that one of the characters
is a Syrian trader, the whole thing might as well be happening in a
London suburb.' The central characters, it is true, are all white
expatriates, but the colonial setting is useful for Greene because
it is an extreme situation (an unbearable combination of heat,
boredom and isolation) which provides hothouse conditions for
the various forms of despair he is exploring. For the whites,
physical alienation is a metaphor for inner alienation; their actual
exile, their separation from their roots and 'nostalgia for something
lost', are all indicative of a more serious spiritual 'shipwreck', to
use the language of *England Made Me*. In the same way, the
vivid sense of wasteland, the seediness and sordidness of their
adopted home (which one might argue, however, is laid on a bit
too thick here, infested as it is with ever-present vultures,
mosquitoes and rats) is used as an image for a world abandoned
by hope and by God.

It is also true that none of the native Africans is fully
developed as a character. They are seen only from the point of
view of the dominant, alien whites, for many of whom all blacks
look alike and are either pimps, prostitutes, 'boys' they cannot
trust or, in the administrators' eyes, relentless and incorrigible

liars. Orwell sees this lack of African characters as a fault, or rather a gap, in the novel, but it should be remembered that the story is narrated from the point of view of the whites who cannot understand or relate to the people any more than they can relate to their country, and that therefore this 'lack' is also part of the point of view. The one exception to this is Scobie, who appreciates the beauty around him, even if it is only the ephemeral, five-minute beauty of a sunset over the laterite roads, 'so ugly and clay-heavy by day', and for whom the country has a fascination beyond its hostile surface: 'The magic of this place never failed him: here he kept his foothold on the very edge of a strange continent.' He has a real affection for the blacks (though it is an undoubtedly paternalistic, colonial affection), especially for his boy, Ali, and the one image of peace in the novel is Scobie's dream at the beginning of Part Three, a dream of 'perfect happiness and freedom . . . walking through a wide cool meadow with Ali at his heels'. It is this affection for the blacks and his love of their country which really separates Scobie from the other expatriates. This same affection makes Scobie's betrayal of Ali the darkest moment of his despair, so that when he finds Ali's dead body, resembling the black beads of a broken rosary he had been looking for, he thinks 'Oh God . . . I've killed you: you've served me all these years and I've killed you at the end of them. God lay there under the petrol drums . . .'

Many of the book's minor characters are sharply and memorably drawn: Wilson, the despicable Intelligence man whose declarations of love for Louise and whose attachment to poetry are used ironically to show his insensitivity and fundamental absurdity; Harris, the true establishment 'white man' figure, trying to keep up his spirits against all the odds by reading the old school magazine and elevating the extermination of cockroaches to a competitive sport; Robinson, the bank manager, maintaining himself by a morbid obsession with ill-health. The exile of these characters from the English provinces, where they belong, has produced a desperation in them which accentuates and reveals their true personalities.

But the English are not the only foreigners in the colony. As Harris observes, 'this is the original Tower of Babel', and it is the

Syrian trader Yusef, the only non-white character in any way developed, who is the most successful, the most 'alive' creation in the novel, comparing himself in stilted English to the base Indian who threw away a pearl, representing greed and corruption yet wanting to talk about the philosophy of life.

The least successful character, on the other hand, is Louise, and this is a real flaw, for in making her such a weak and neurotic person, unlovable and impossible to live with, the force of Scobie's dilemma is weakened. 'Here was a technical fault rather than a psychological one,' writes Greene in *Ways of Escape*:

Louise Scobie is mainly seen through the eyes of Scobie, and we have no chance of revising our opinion of her. Helen, the girl whom Scobie loves, gains an unfair advantage.

The only scene in which Louise shows any independence of mind is during her walk with Wilson along the abandoned railway track when she turns on him with: 'For God's sake don't be humble'. In the first editions of the book Greene omitted this passage, thinking it slackened the pace and detracted the reader's attention away from Scobie. Later, however, realizing the bias in the novel against Louise and seeing this omission as only aggravating it, he reinserted the passage, commenting: 'By eliminating it I thought I gained intensity and impetus, but I had sacrificed tone.'

In *Ways of Escape* Greene expresses a low opinion of *The Heart of the Matter*, claiming that he was 'out of practice and out of confidence' after a five-year break from novel writing. He also leads the reader, in a vague, inscrutable passage, to assume that the book's tone of unrelenting pessimism was the expression of an emotional crisis in his personal life, when his own thoughts ran to suicide. Indeed, the following sentence, from *Ways of Escape*, could easily have come from Scobie's lips:.

I had always thought that war would bring death as a solution in one form or another, in the blitz, in a submarined ship, in Africa with a dose of blackwater, but here I was alive, the carrier of unhappiness to people I loved . . .

The Heart of the Matter is perhaps the novel Greene himself most dislikes among his work, apart from the two early books that he suppressed. He admits that his dislike of it may be due to the private memories of 'personal anguish' it holds for him, but, acute critic of his own work as he always is, he realizes that despite its having been the novel which more than any other established his reputation as a serious writer, and despite its considerable technical merits, it represents his least successful attempt to deal with Catholic themes in fiction.

II

In 'At Home', an essay on the Blitz written in 1940, Greene wrote:

There are things one never gets used to because they don't connect: sanctity and fidelity and the courage of human beings abandoned to free will: virtues like these belong with old college buildings and cathedrals, relics of a world with faith.

As far back as *The Man Within* (1929) Greene displayed an awkwardness with 'sanctity and fidelity' and a corresponding facility for describing the corruption and violence of a fallen world. Violence, Greene wrote, satisfied a 'moral craving for the just and reasonable expression of human nature left without belief', so that life in the Blitz, that universal violence which seemed like the 'breaking' of 'an old dog-toothed civilization', became 'just and poetic'.

The Blitz was used as the background in *The Ministry of Fear* to emphasize the sensational, melodramatic nature of modern life in a world 'remade by William Le Queux'. In *The End of the Affair* it is the setting for the mysterious actions of a God who, to use the terminology of the novel, 'seduces' His sinners to believe in Him, so that, in the midst of total violence, 'sanctity and fidelity and the courage of human beings' are rediscovered.

The story is narrated by Maurice Bendrix, a novelist whose affair with Sarah Miles is inexplicably and suddenly brought to an end by her after the house they are in is bombed and he himself has a narrow escape from death. Bewildered by Sarah's withdrawal, Bendrix assumes that she has found another lover. He does nothing, however, until eighteen months later, when he meets Henry, Sarah's husband, who has belatedly become suspicious of his wife's behaviour, and he maliciously undertakes to have her followed on Henry's behalf.

Parkis, the private detective he hires, obtains Sarah's private journal and discovers that at the moment of the bombing she had been convinced that Bendrix had been killed and had instinctively prayed to a God in whom she had no belief, promising to end her adulterous affair with Bendrix if God gave him back his life: 'and then he came in at the door, and he was alive, and I thought now the agony of being without him starts . . .'

Despite herself, Sarah is forced by what she sees as a miracle to believe in God and she painfully keeps her vow to give up Bendrix. To try to convince herself that the 'miracle' of Bendrix's survival is in fact only due to coincidence and superstition, Sarah attends regular sessions with Richard Smythe, an atheist with an intense intellectual hatred of God and a self-proclaimed mission to convert others to disbelief. This serves only to fuel Bendrix's suspicions, however, and to strengthen Sarah's ever-deepening faith.

This was the first novel in which Greene used the first-person technique, though he had recently experimented with it in the screenplay of *The Third Man*. For a writer so concerned as Greene with maintaining point of view, the first-person offers a considerable technical advantage, for it insures against 'any temptation to deviate – "I" could only observe what "I" observed' (*WE*). However, after having embarked on the book, Greene regretted the use of the first person with its unforseen problems, such as how to vary 'the all-important "tone" when it was one character who was always commenting'. In an attempt to solve this he created a book within a book, Sarah's diary, which supplies the answer to the mystery of her secret love and also counters Bendrix's chronicle of hatred ('This is a record of hate far more than of love') with a softer, though equally painful tone.

Bendrix's narrative is intimate, conversational, direct, evidence of a witty and urbane personality who not only tells the story but lives it, and it is an extremely successful use of the first person by Greene. However, in Sarah's own first-person account, the technique fails and her diary reads as stilted and contrived. Greene, like Conrad, has difficulty in portraying convincing women characters, but the main problem here is that whereas Bendrix is concerned in his account with action as well as thought, Sarah is concerned only with rationalization. Her progression from willing adulteress to reluctant saint is a process of thought and feeling which is reported in her diary. She explains this progress, but we do not *see* it happening, with the result that it has none of the directness or intensity of Bendrix's jealousy, suspicion and hatred. It is perhaps the fact that Bendrix is a novelist which enables Greene to re-create his psychological workings so successfully (many of Bendrix's comments on the art of the novel echo Greene's own). However, it is ironic that while in life, which for Bendrix is the 'grand plot' drawn up by God, the master novelist, it is only the saints who are 'living characters', who 'move and speak', in Greene's own creation it is not the saint but the non-believer who actually comes alive for the reader.

Bendrix's atheistic account of the affair is dominated by physical details: his body in the mirror; the hairs on Sarah's back; her 'brown, indeterminate-coloured hair like a pool of liquor on the parquet'; the physical sensation and release of human love; Henry's bald patch (most of the characters suffer from and are humilated by imperfect bodies: bald patches, ugly birth marks, lameness, even coughs and colds). Sarah in her account is also very sensitive to the physical side of life but she attempts to go beneath the skin, and longs to escape the physical by relief in 'a vapour':

I was trying to escape from the human body and all it needed. I thought I could believe in some kind of a God that bore no relation to ourselves, something vague, amorphous, cosmic . . . like a powerful vapour moving among the chairs and walls. One day I too would become part of that vapour – I would escape myself for ever.

However, Sarah's capacity to love God proceeds directly from her love of Bendrix. In *Brighton Rock* it was suggested that the experience of physical love could offer a way of salvation for Pinkie, though this idea was not enlarged upon; in *The End of the Affair*, however, it becomes one of the main themes. It is through human, carnal love that Sarah comes to experience divine love, which is why Sarah can only believe in a physical, material God, who is portrayed as a divine lover, as Bendrix's rival for Sarah's heart:

Did I ever love Maurice as much before I loved You? Or was it really You I loved all the time? Did I touch You when I touched him? Could I have touched You if I hadn't touched him first, touched him as I never touched Henry, anybody? And he loved me and touched me as he never did any other woman. But was it me he loved, or You?

Rather in the manner of the Old Testament, several of Greene's characters strike bargains with God, which He keeps: not only Sarah, but the whisky priest in *The Power and the Glory*, Scobie in *The Heart of the Matter* and Father Callifer in the play, *The Potting Shed*. God's activity in the world extends further in this novel, however, by the performance of miracles through the medium of His saint, Sarah, whose 'cure' of Smythe's skin blemish and of the Parkis boy's illness seem designed mainly for their effect on Bendrix, who at the end is left fighting belief despite the evidence before his own eyes. Sarah even intermediates in the answer of his own 'prayer', in the crematorium, to 'save' Sylvia from being seduced by him: 'But if I start believing that, then I have to believe in your God. I'd have to love your God. I'd rather love the men you slept with.' Bendrix hates God for His interference in the world, for His spoiling human happiness in taking Sarah away from him, and this very hatred is a paradoxical form of belief, as he himself is aware:

I wanted something very simple and very easy: I wanted Sarah for a lifetime and You took her away. With Your great schemes You ruin our happiness like a harvester ruins a mouse's nest: I hate You God, I hate You as though You existed.

Greene portrays Bendrix's rational, anti-God point of view, as well as his slow reluctant progress towards doubt of his atheism, with great force and sympathy. The narrator's firm disbelief also makes his account of Sarah's conversion, incorporating as it does many elements of mystery or detective fiction, wholly convincing: the sceptic makes a more persuasive hagiographer than the propagandist.

Some critics and readers have found the portrayal of God and miracles to be out of place in a realist novel, and in particular they have criticized the 'supernatural' implications of Sarah's secret baptism into the Catholic Church as a child, which 'took' mysteriously 'like vaccination'. But there seems no real argument against this 'supernaturalism', for if the novel is dealing with a religion which has its foundations in the divine answering of prayer and the performance of miracles, it seems unreasonable to demand that in fiction (where anything can legitimately happen anyway) this religion should be portrayed without its magical aspect. Evelyn Waugh, reviewing the novel in *The Month*, applauded this 'defiant assertion of the supernatural' and wrote:

His earlier books tended to show Catholics to themselves and set them puzzling. *The End of the Affair* is addressed to the Gentiles. It shows the Church as something in their midst, mysterious and triumphant and working for their good. One might say that in places it is too emphatically sectarian.

Waugh, like others, saw *The End of the Affair* as the most Catholic of Greene's novels, but it is also one of his most unorthodox. Indeed, Waugh is quite incorrect in saying that it shows the Church as 'something in our midst', for it is the person of God, and definitely not the Church, who is seen as 'mysterious and triumphant'. It is a story in which sainthood is achieved through the sin of adultery (in a church whose female saints are almost exclusively virgins); in which the saint accuses priests of being 'between us and God'; and in which the theological speculations and wranglings of the Church are seen by Sarah in her letter to Bendrix as irrelevant to belief, in a way which anticipates the denunciation of philosophical and moral theology in 'A Visit to Morin' and *A Burnt-Out Case*:

But what's the good, Maurice? I believe there's a God – I believe the whole bag of tricks, there's nothing I don't believe, they could subdivide the Trinity into a dozen parts and I'd believe . . . I've fallen into belief like I fell in love.

After writing *The Heart of the Matter* and *The Third Man*, Greene, by now middle-aged and successful, faced a crisis not only in his personal life, as mentioned earlier, but also in his artistic life. He explained in *Ways of Escape*:

Writing a novel does not become easier with practice. The slow discovery by a novelist of his individual method can be exciting, but a moment comes in middle age when he feels that he no longer controls his method; he has become its prisoner. Then a long period of ennui sets in: it seems to him he has done everything before. He is more afraid to read his favourable critics than his unfavourable, for with terrible patience they unroll before his eyes the unchanging pattern of the carpet.

The End of the Affair was in some respects an attempt to break free of 'the method' and to change direction by replacing melodrama with domestic romance and tragedy, but it shows an even deeper involvement with Catholic themes than earlier novels, with its miracles and saint and the conversion of an atheist. Philip Stratford in *Faith and Fiction* claims that it comes closer than any of the other novels 'to an out-and-out demonstration of faith', while J. D. Scott, reviewing it for *The New Statesman*, attacked Greene's 'narrowness' and gibed that this was the last novel a non-specialist, or layman, would be able to review. Commenting on this in the *Paris Review* interview, Greene predicted that *The End of the Affair* would mark the end of his Catholic phase. It was, he said, a cycle that was now complete and his next novel would not 'deal explicitly with Catholic themes at all'.

The next novel, *The Quiet American*, does indeed have a political rather than a religious emphasis. Its hero, Fowler, shares Bendrix's cynical attitude to religion, but this time there are no miracles to force him to question his lack of belief, and God is no longer seen as an active force in the world. However, ten years after *The End of the Affair* and six years after *The Quiet American*, Greene returned to explore specifically Catholic themes in *A Burnt-Out Case*, so that this book stands as a sort of epilogue to the so-called Catholic phase of his fiction, and for this reason it is discussed in the present chapter along with his other religious novels.

III

In *A Burnt-Out Case*, the 'hollow man' Querry, a famous Church architect who has lost his faith, tells a story about a King's Jeweller. This 'fable' has dominated much discussion of the book, for it is not only a thinly veiled allegory of Querry's life but also seems to relate strongly to Greene's own feelings at the time, with regard to his reputation as a Catholic novelist.

In the fable the 'hero' realizes that 'he was not born to be an artist at all: only a very clever jeweller'. He has won praise for his expert craftsmanship, making complicated jewels in the form of a golden egg with a figure holding another egg inside, which opened to reveal another figure with an egg, and so on. And as on the top of each egg 'there was a gold cross set with clips of precious stones in honour of the King', who of course is God, 'he was highly praised too for the seriousness of his subject matter.' This is an obvious reference to Greene's Catholic novels, for like Querry he too has felt worn out 'with the ingenuity of his design' and worn out by critics who all 'said much the same thing'.

As we have seen, *The End of the Affair* was an initial attempt to break what Greene refers to (in the words of Henry James) as the 'pattern of the carpet' (see page 94). During the 1950s, he made several more attempts, as we shall see in Chapter Six, but it is perhaps only with *A Burnt-Out Case* that he finally freed himself from the straitjacket of his style and his reputation. His need to do so became urgent after the 'great vulgar success' of *The Heart of the Matter*, as a result of which he was approached by an over-whelming number of people, mostly women and priests, who burdened him with their spiritual problems, so that the Church seemed to him like 'a village struck with plague'. The desperation of so many 'believers' had a profound effect on him and led directly to the writing of *A Burnt-Out Case*:

I felt myself used and exhausted by the victims of religion. The vision of faith as an untroubled sea was lost for ever; faith was more like a tempest in which the lucky were engulfed and lost, and the unfortunate survived to be flung battered and bleeding on the shore . . . I had no apostolic mission, and the cries for spiritual assistance maddened me because of my impotence. What was the Church for but to aid these sufferers? What was the priesthood for? I was like a man without medical knowledge in a village struck with plague. It was in those years, I think, that Querry was born, and Father Thomas too [the troubled priest in *A Burnt-Out Case*]. He had often sat in that chair of mine, and he had worn many faces.

(*WE*)

Readers of *A Burnt-Out Case* and the short story which preceded it, 'A Visit to Morin', suspected a crisis in Greene's own faith. Some, most notably his friend and fellow Catholic Evelyn Waugh, even thought that he must have lost faith altogether. Morin is a 'Catholic writer', like Greene, who tells a young admirer that he has lost his 'belief', though not his 'faith': 'Perhaps I wrote away my belief like the young man writes away his love.' This distinction between 'belief' and 'faith' is an important one in Greene's work. Faith for Greene means an unquestioning acceptance of God and a trust in His love and mercy. Belief, on the other hand, is man's rationalization and institutionalization of God, through theology and the Church. In *The Other Man* Greene revealed that some time before writing *The End of the Affair* he had himself experienced a crisis of belief though had kept his faith, like Morin. Also like Morin he had 'excommunicated' himself:

In my private life, my situation is not regular. If I went to Communion, I would have to confess and make promises. I prefer to excommunicate myself. That's why I said, at a conference in Paris with Mauriac, that I could only speak in the name of the 'semi-lapsed' . . .

If I don't believe in X or Y, faith intervenes, telling me I'm wrong not to believe. Faith is above belief. One can say that it's a gift of God, while belief is not. Belief is founded on reason. On the whole I keep my faith while enduring long periods of disbelief.

The problem of belief for Greene is that it is founded on the 'unconvincing philosophical arguments' of theologians. A distrust of theology recurs throughout Greene's work, and is best summed up by Morin:

A man can accept anything to do with God until scholars begin to go into the details and the implications. A man can accept the Trinity, but the arguments that follow . . . I would never try to determine some point in differential calculus with a two-times-two table. You end by disbelieving the calculus.

In *A Burnt-Out Case* Querry, who was once part of the Catholic establishment, has lost not only his belief but also his faith, both in God and in man. In a moment of emotional and spiritual crisis he suddenly 'disappears' to a remote African leper colony where he finds a group of missionaries struggling against the odds to minister to the physical and spiritual needs of the lepers. The priests are assisted by Dr Colin, an atheist, yet a man of great humanity and compassion. During his stay at the *leproserie* Querry begins to 'recover', as he rediscovers a reason for living by joining the doctor and the Fathers in their work. However, near the colony lives Rycker, a frustrated, bitter man who has in the past failed in an attempt to become a priest and now suffers from what can only be called a spiritual inferiority complex. Querry feels sorry for Rycker's pathetic, lonely and long-suffering wife, Marie, and tries to help her face up to the petty tyranny of her husband. Rycker, however, though at first overly impressed by the fame of '*the* Querry', suspects him (without reason) of having seduced his wife, and the novel ends with Rycker arriving at the *leproserie* in a jealous rage, armed with a gun. Querry laughs at the absurdity of the whole misunderstanding, but Rycker, thinking he is laughing at him, shoots him dead.

Laughter, or the lack of it, is a symptom of Querry's 'sickness', that of having 'no more interest in life at all'. On his way to the *leproserie* at the beginning of the novel the laughter of others irritates him and he wonders 'when it was that he had first begun to detest laughter like a bad smell'. He himself is incapable of laughing, until he slowly starts to move towards 'recovery' when he learns like the doctor and the Fathers to 'serve other people'. Then at first he makes 'an odd awkward sound', which the doctor interprets as an attempt to laugh, but when finally confronted by the armed Rycker he laughs outright, for the first time – and thus he dies laughing, or rather he dies because he laughs.

A Burnt-Out Case is a further example of Greene's ability to unite setting with subject matter. The leper colony is sketched briefly but vividly and convincingly, without sensationalism or sentimentalism. It provides a metaphor for Querry's spiritual state: like one of the 'burnt-out' lepers who has reached the stage of the disease where mutilation is an 'alternative to pain', he is spiritually mutilated by having lost his faith and his sense of hope. The *leproserie* is a closed environment, a means of isolating a number of characters from the outside world. It is also Greene's most extreme setting, a place of poverty and sickness, misery and despair. But within the darkest corner of 'Greeneland', goodness and charity are seen to flourish, and despite Querry's death the story is not entirely pessimistic, as we shall see.

In the characters of Querry, Rycker, Dr Colin and the priests, Greene explores various degrees and states of belief and disbelief. He himself comments on this in *Ways of Escape*:

The doctor, whom I like best as a realized character, represents a settled and easy atheism; the Father Superior a settled and easy belief (I use easy as a term of praise and not as a term of reproach); Father Thomas an unsettled form of belief and Querry an unsettled form of disbelief.

We have moved here far away from Péguy's bad citizen and good stranger, as found in *Brighton Rock*, for by far the most sympathetic character in *A Burnt-Out Case* is the atheist, Dr Colin. Ironically, it is he who understands Querry's spiritual dilemma better than any of the priests in the *leproserie*. He is dedicated to curing man's physical ailments and although he has no philosophy to live by, he believes in a form of spiritual evolution going on 'inside the brains of man' ('We are riding a great ninth evolutionary wave'), which clearly suggests that he has been influenced by the evolutionary theories of Teilhard de Chardin, as Greene himself had (*ASOL*). Despite his atheism the doctor is 'religious' in his concern for man and in his metaphysical ponderings on man's origins and spiritual state (even his rationalism is seen as a form of 'superstition', like the beliefs of the Fathers). In *The Other Man* Greene calls him 'more mystical' than the priests, which links him to that other mystical atheist, the police lieutenant in *The Power and the Glory*. Dr Colin, however, is a better man than the lieutenant, more understanding and tolerant (he does not hate God, like the lieutenant, but simply does not believe in Him), and his crusade is the practical, realizable one of curing lepers rather than an impossible fight for universal justice. The main difference between them as characters is that Colin is a reasonable man, not an idealist or an extremist.

Rycker and Father Thomas, the extremist Catholics in the novel, are 'victims' of religion in whom belief has the upper hand over faith, and Father Thomas inflicts his own spiritual and psychological problems on Querry just as real-life priests did on

Greene. The other priests of the colony, however, are treated with greater sympathy than any other of Greene's clerical charac- ters, with the sole exception of Monsignor Quixote. They are shown as good rather than holy men, concerned with the practi- calities of building and raising money for the hospital rather than with the niceties of moral theology, or 'what the Church considered sin'. The only one who has not managed, like Father Jean, 'to wipe out an ugly past' of theology is Father Thomas, who is still attached to the arguments of the seminary as if 'damned to a perpetual and unhappy youth'. The others, by comparison, are mature adults who get on with life: '. . . men who had grown up and were more concerned over the problems of the electric-light plant or the quality of the brickmaking . . .'

Querry learns from the missionaries' example and gradually moves away from the state of 'total vacancy' towards 'recovery', towards a new reason for living and a settled form of belief or disbelief. It is clear that he would in the end be 'cured', but before then the absurdity of life intervenes. It is the absurd, grotesque characters – Rycker, Father Thomas and the journalist Parkinson – who try to prevent his recovery, because of their stupidity and because they all have a vested interest in his suffer- ing, in having a saint or a new Schweitzer in their midst. Rycker, the failed priest, wants someone of importance (and '*the* Querry' is certainly that) to understand his spiritual problems and thus give importance to them ('He can't bear not being important'). Father Thomas, on the other hand, finds in Querry an image of humility, and uses him to bolster his own lagging faith. Like Rycker, Father Thomas stupidly and obstinately misunderstands Querry, insisting on his own interpretation of Querry's state of mind:

'We both of us have our doubts,' Father Thomas said. 'Perhaps I have more than you. They even come to me at the altar with the Host in my hands.'

'I've long ceased to have doubts. Father, if I must speak plainly, I don't believe at all. Not at all. I've worked it out of my system – like women. I've no desire to convert others to disbelief, or even to worry them. I want to keep my mouth shut, if only you'd let me.'

'You can't think what a lot of good our conversation has done me . . .

One sometimes desperately needs a man who has experienced the same weaknesses as oneself.'

'But you've misunderstood me, father.'

'Don't you see that perhaps you've been given the grace of aridity? Perhaps even now you are walking in the footsteps of St. John of the Cross, the *noche oscura*.'

Rycker and Father Thomas are shown to be, in their spiritual preoccupations, egotistical and self-indulgent, and significantly it is Father Thomas who is the first to believe Rycker's incredible libel against Querry, that he had seduced his wife Marie.

The third absurd figure to prevent Querry from recovery is Parkinson, one of a long line of journalists in Greene's fiction, from Mabel Warren in *Stamboul Train* on, who 'make history' not according to the truth as they see it, but according to their own psychological needs. Parkinson is a vivid character, comical yet at the same time menacing. He is ridiculous and pathetic as a man, but has the power to convince three million readers of the *Post* of whatever he likes. So it is that he decides to 'make' Querry at first a popular saint, by the articles he writes about him, and then after he has himself engineered the scandal of the night spent with Marie, to make him 'the saint who failed'.

Greene breaks 'the pattern' in this book by shifting absurdity and comedy, which until now have only made brief appearances in the serious novels, centre stage at the moment of high serious-ness. Farcical as they are, Rycker, Parkinson and Father Thomas all have the power to interfere in Querry's life and to destroy it. That Querry's downfall is brought about by a suspected adultery with the unappealing Marie is heavily ironic: he had been promis-cuous in the past, yet with Marie he had only been trying to defend and help her, so though he had technically 'spent the night' with her, they had not in fact been lovers. The whole situation – one of silly domestic farce – trivializes any possible sense of tragedy. Father Jean likens the situation to a Palais Royal farce, and his argument with Father Thomas about God's sense of humour points forward to Brown's idea of the 'authori-tative practical joker' in *The Comedians*:

'Sometimes I think God was not entirely serious when he gave man the sexual instinct.'

'If that is one of the doctrines you teach in moral theology . . .'
'Nor when he invented moral theology.'

Just before Rycker shoots, Brother Philippe suggests they all
need a cold shower, 'and as though to illustrate his words, a
waterfall of rain suddenly descended on them.' It is a final parody
of divine intervention. God is not with them as Querry dies
laughing, saying 'Absurd . . . this is absurd or else . . .' He had
been laughing at himself, at life, perhaps at the cold shower, but
not at Rycker; it is life which is absurd and although the deliberately ambiguous and tantalizing 'or else' has led some critics to
assume a final move back to faith, Dr Colin, who is the one to
understand Querry best, warns against such a conclusion: 'Oh
no, not that.'

The last words of the novel are given to the Father Superior
and the doctor, the 'whole' men who are untormented by their
belief or disbelief. Unlike the other Catholic novels, there is no
mention here of God's mercy nor any invitation to the reader to
speculate on the hero's fate after death. After the funeral they
simply get back to work, having already 'wasted enough time on
the dead'. At the beginning of the novel the Father Superior had
said, 'it would be a good thing for all of us if we were even more
superficial', and he echoes this at the end by warning that 'we all
analyse motives too much'. For him the doubt and despair of
Querry are avoided by not looking too deeply; by not delving
into those questions which man is ultimately incapable of answering; by trusting God and by getting on with the work of charity,
with helping to fight injustice and suffering which is the role of
the individual Christian in this life and which in Greene's next
book, *The Comedians*, takes on a political dimension.

6 Comedy and Commitment

In Chapter Six of *Ways of Escape* Greene tells how the 1950s were for him a period of great unrest:

I was in that mood for escape which comes, I suppose, to most men in middle life, though with me it arrived early, even in childhood – escape from boredom, escape from depression. If I had been a bank clerk, I would have dreamed of betraying my trust and absconding to South America.

This desire for change and escape inevitably shows itself in his work. Many of Greene's later heroes are middle-aged men trying to make a similar escape: Querry in *A Burnt-Out Case*, Wormold in *Our Man in Havana*, Henry Pulling in *Travels with My Aunt* and even, to an extent, Monsignor Quixote. There is also a restless experimenting with different techniques throughout the 1950s, a decade which includes three plays and a considerable number of short stories.

Travel was another form of escape taken by Greene at this time, and it became a habit with him 'to visit troubled places, not to seek material for novels but to regain the sense of insecurity which I had enjoyed in three blitzes on London' (*WE*).

This search for danger and 'insecurity' led Greene to Kenya during the Mau Mau rebellion; to Malaya during the Emergency; to Vietnam during the French war; to Cuba under Batista's rule; to Poland under Stalin, as well as to a leper colony in the Belgian Congo. Out of these 'escapes' into danger during the 1950s three novels emerged: *The Quiet American*, set in Vietnam; *Our Man in Havana*, set in Cuba; and *A Burnt-Out Case*, set in the Congo.

Much of Greene's travelling has been undertaken as a journalist, but he has always been careful to separate novel writing and journalism, just as he has always been careful to separate his own political views and those of his characters, as he told Philip Toynbee in an interview for the *Observer* (15 September 1957): 'If anyone has anything to say about society or politics, let him say it as journalism.'

It was as a journalist that Greene went to Vietnam and, as he himself points out in *Ways of Escape,* there is more 'direct reportage' in *The Quiet American* than in any other of his novels, though this reportage is rescued from any sense of extraneousness by the fact that Fowler, the first-person narrator, is a foreign correspondent for a London newspaper and sees Vietnam from a journalist's point of view.

After the complexity of *The End of the Affair,* which chronologically it follows, the subject matter and language of *The Quiet American* are comparatively simple. The actual structure, however, with its numerous time shifts, is as complex as any of the other novels. The novel opens, and closes, with the political assassination of an idealistic young American official, Pyle, at the hands of a mysterious Communist 'Committee' led by Mr Heng. What comes in between is the reconstruction, in Fowler's mind, of the events leading up to the murder.

Pyle and Fowler represent opposite values in a dialogue between innocence and experience, ideology and doubt, idealism and realism. Pyle has come to the war in Vietnam full of ideological theories about the politics of the situation – in particular, the need for a 'third force' in the struggle. He is, however, a dangerous innocent stumbling around a political minefield. With his government's backing he finds, and finances, this third force in an unscrupulous mercenary, General Thé, whose first action is to explode a 'bicycle bomb' in a crowded square, killing and maiming a number of innocent bystanders. It is at this point that Fowler, who until then has been resolutely avoiding any political involvement, feels he must act to prevent Pyle from putting any more of his policies into action, and he cooperates with Heng in the planning of Pyle's murder. Fowler's political motives are confused with his personal feelings, however, for Pyle has recently robbed him of his Annamite mistress, Phuong.

With *The Quiet American* Greene returned to the political subjects he had first dealt with in *It's a Battlefield.* Here, as in the early novels, it is the relationship between the world of the individual and the public world we all inhabit which interests him. However, the main characters in *The Quiet American,* unlike those of the earlier political novels, are not unexpectedly and reluctantly caught up in events, but are involved by choice. Like Greene, they have taken return tickets to danger and enjoy a sort of Olympian detachment, a detachment which enables Fowler to report both sides of the war as he sees it and Pyle to view the situation as an opportunity to put his academic theories into practice.

The main theme of the novel is commitment. Pyle, through his belief in democracy and liberalism, is committed to positive action. He is a political missionary (literally part of the U.S. 'Economic Aid Mission') 'absorbed . . . in the responsibilities of the West'. Fowler, on the other hand, has washed his hands of politics, and is the first of a number of Greene's characters who consciously cultivate a philosophy of non-involvement:

'I'm not involved,' I repeated. It had been an article of my creed. The human condition being what it was, let them fight, let them love, let them murder, I would not be involved. My fellow journalists called themselves correspondents; I preferred the title of reporter. I wrote what I saw. I took no action – even an opinion is a kind of action.

Fowler's narrative, however, is a statement of how this detachment is eroded as he realizes that even though the 'responsibilities of the West' mean nothing to him, it is impossible to avoid individual responsibility if at the same time one loves people or cares what happens to them.

The central scene in the book is the night Fowler and Pyle pass together in the watchtower, hiding from Vietminh snipers, with two frightened Vietnamese peasant soldiers. This, the most exciting and well-written part of the story, combines a very real sense of danger and fear with a terse dialogue exposing their opposing attitudes to life. When the tower is attacked they manage to escape, with Pyle saving Fowler's life. At this moment Fowler becomes aware of one of the soldiers crying in the dark, wounded and in pain, and realizes that despite himself he has become involved and is responsible for another's pain and suffering – for the soldier would have surrendered if they had not forced him at the point of a gun to stay:

> I had prided myself on detachment, on not belonging to this war, but those wounds had been inflicted by me just as though I had used the sten, as Pyle wanted me to do.
>   I made an effort to get over the bank into the road. I wanted to join him. It was the only thing I could do, to share his pain.

Fowler's compassion for the suffering of innocent victims had been aroused earlier at Phat Diem, when he had seen the canal full of bodies, 'human beings, not just grey drained cadavers', and the small child shot in the arms of his mother, an image which returns to haunt him as the French plane he is in arbitrarily and casually strafes a sampan on the Yellow River. It is this witnessing of individual suffering which leads Fowler to 'hate war', and ultimately to become involved by collaborating in the murder of Pyle. Sooner or later, Heng had told him, 'one has to take sides . . . if one is to remain human', and this reminded him of Captain Trouin in the opium house, who on being shown a picture of Phuong, Fowler's mistress, had predicted that 'one day something will happen, you will take a side'. This is ironic because in the event Fowler's motives for taking sides are ambiguous, tinged with personal revenge against Pyle for taking Phuong away from him.

Although Phuong is the only fully developed Vietnamese character in the novel, she is a shadowy figure whom we never really understand, a curious blend of innocence and experience which makes her a new creation in Greene's fiction. She has the thinness and fragility of the earlier Rose/Coral stock characters, but has greater strength and a natural sensuousness which is not immoral, an eroticism which is not corrupt. She is a 'natural' woman, although her thought processes are straightforward and uncomplicated to a point which strains credibility. Fowler compares her and the other Vietnamese to children:

> '. . . It's a cliché to call them children – but there's one thing which is childish. They love you in return for kindness, security, the presents you give them – they hate you for a blow or an injustice. They don't know

what it's like – just walking into a room and loving a stranger. For an
ageing man, Pyle, it's very secure – she won't run away from home so
long as the home is happy.'

Despite Fowler's compassion for the Vietnamese as individuals,
as characters in his narrative they have very little individuality
and are portrayed for the most part as innocent victims of the
war, very often dead victims. He has a rather patronizing attitude
towards them, though not the same feeling of superiority that
Pyle displays in thinking he knows what is best for them. Pyle's
confidence in assuming responsibility for the affairs of others is a
result of his goodness and his 'innocence'. But the price of Pyle's
innocence – his dream of helping the Vietnamese people by
imposing his abstract theories on them – is further suffering and
death.

At the beginning of the novel Fowler says to Vigot, the 'priest-
like' detective investigating Pyle's death: 'God save us always
from the innocent and good'. But Pyle is not innocent in the way
the Vietnamese are innocent – victims of a violent world beyond
their control. He is a stranger in the country with little experience
of the world, let alone Vietnam, who has 'studied the East on
paper', notably in the textbooks of the imaginary political theorist
York Harding. His innocence, therefore, is the result of ignorance
and conditioning, a lack of moral education for which Fowler, in
an outburst to Pyle's American boss, blames his social and cul-
tural background. Pyle is a product of his society, a victim of its
beliefs and its prejudices, and therefore, like Pinkie in *Brighton
Rock,* he cannot be held fully responsible for his actions:

'They killed him because he was too innocent to live. He was young and
ignorant and silly and he got involved. He had no more of a notion than
any of you what the whole affair's about, and you gave him money and
York Harding's books on the East and said, "Go ahead. Win the East
for Democracy." He never saw anything he hadn't heard in a lecture-
hall, and his writers and his lecturers made a fool of him. When he saw a
dead body he couldn't even see the wounds. A Red Menace, a soldier of
democracy.'

With Pyle's political mission to Vietnam Greene developed the
Jamesian theme of New World innocence at large in the Old

World to include the developments of twentieth-century international politics and in particular the U.S. policy of involvement in the internal affairs of other countries. But the indictment against Pyle is not just a political one against U.S. foreign policy, though Fowler is opposed to the new 'liberal' colonialism just as he disapproves of the British colonial past. It is a moral indictment of the whole world view, the black-and-white philosophy of life that leads men to believe in liberal colonialism, or democracy, or any other abstraction as a cause worth fighting for and worth sacrificing the happiness and lives of others for.

When *The Quiet American* first appeared Greene was, not surprisingly, criticized for his anti-Americanism (though after subsequent events in Vietnam this criticism was drowned by praise of his political foresight). The anti-American charge centred on the fact that Greene seemed to dislike Pyle for what he is as much as for what he does, and the other Americans in the story, in particular the journalist Granger, are also profoundly unlikeable. There is a danger here of confusing the author with his fictional creation, for Greene is not Fowler any more than he is Pinkie or Scobie, and nor are Fowler's opinions necessarily his own. It is also clear that he is as critical of Fowler's detachment as he is of Pyle's interference, and while it is true that on several occasions outside the pages of the novel he has expressed extreme distaste for American consumerism and liberalism, as well as for the country's foreign policy, it would be simplistic to confuse this with racial snobbery or hatred.

The novel, too, is far more complex than that. Fowler's prejudices are carefully declared at the beginning, establishing him as an unreliable narrator. His motives for betraying Pyle are ambiguous and politically 'unreliable'. Similarly, Pyle is not the 'straw target' Terry Eagleton has called him. Although Fowler's picture is biased, he acknowledges of Pyle that he 'never knew a man who had better motives for all the trouble he caused' (and Greene has stated elsewhere his belief that we are saved or damned by our motives rather than our actions). Pyle is also seen as decisive and heroic, and is even responsible for saving Fowler's life. As in real life, the theoretical issues in the story are confused by the contradictions of personality and motive. Pyle has good qualities which are undeniable, whereas Fowler is selfish and indecisive;

Pyle's motives for action are pure and objective, Fowler's are ambiguous and personal. Fowler's very involvement is a form of corruption, leading as it does to the betrayal of Pyle's trust and the abetment of his murder. Pyle, on the other hand, is guiltless: '. . . you can't blame the innocent, they are always guiltless. All you can do is control them or eliminate them.' Ignorance and good motivation extenuate the harm caused by innocence which, Fowler concludes, 'is a kind of insanity'. He realizes at the end that he too is guilty of ignorance, when he finds compassion even for the suffering of the journalist Granger whom until then he has despised. He asks himself: 'Am I so different from Pyle? . . . Must I too have my foot thrust in the mess of life before I saw the pain?'

In recounting his trip to Kenya in *Ways of Escape* Greene wrote, 'We have lost the power of clear action because we have lost the ability to believe.' Pyle does not have that indecision which Greene considers to be 'part of the modern mind'. On the contrary, he is too ready to make a decision with insufficient knowledge and forethought, a decision based only on 'belief'. What he believes in is the American dream, a dream of democracy and liberalism, but he has a similarly confident, unquestioning belief in God: 'Things to us wouldn't make sense without Him.'

Fowler, on the other hand, has no belief in anything except the finality of death, which will at least end his fear of losing happiness or losing love – the shadow over even his happiest moments. Like Scobie in *The Heart of the Matter,* Querry in *A Burnt-Out Case,* and Castle in *The Human Factor,* he is looking for 'peace of mind', but finds it only in the ephemeral reveries of an opium-induced trance. Fowler's spiritual doubts lead to his philosophy of detachment, his refusal to be *engagé,* but at the end the 'mess of life' and the heartless activities of Pyle against people Fowler sees as individuals force him to take a stand. This sense of compassion and acceptance of responsibility demonstrate his essential humanity, though the form of commitment he displays has no religious dimension, as it was to have in Greene's later novels. On the contrary, Fowler is cynical about religious belief: 'No human being will ever understand another,' he writes, 'perhaps that's why men have invented God – a being capable of understanding.' If he himself felt the need to be understood, then he too would 'bamboozle' himself into belief. At the end, however, his atheistic certainty begins to give way: he offers Pyle's God the chance to intervene, in a half-hearted attempt to transfer the blame for his treachery:

I handed back the decision to that Somebody in whom I didn't believe: You can intervene if You want to: a telegram on his desk: a message from the Minister. You cannot exist unless you have the power to alter the future.

After Pyle's death everything 'goes right' with Fowler but his conscience is not clear and he wishes there existed 'someone to whom I could say I was sorry', which is the first time he exhibits 'the need for understanding'. This has led some critics to speculate that he is moving towards faith, though such a conclusion has no supporting textual evidence.

II

As Greene recounts in *Ways of Escape,* after finishing the book about Vietnam, the mood of 'escape' was still on him and he spent several weeks in Monte Carlo, living in a luxurious hotel and gambling at the Casino. He went there with the intention not only of enjoying himself but also of researching the background for what he hoped would prove to be

an amusing, agreeably sentimental *novella* – something which neither my friends nor my enemies would expect. It was to be called *Loser Takes All.* A reputation is like a death mask. I wanted to smash the mask.

Loser Takes All bears most resemblance to Greene's short stories: a few characters, a limited number of settings, a simplicity of language and theme, and a clear sense of unity. It is the expression of a single, light mood, an amusing escape from reality for both reader and author. The nature of that escape is inextricably linked to the subject matter of the book – gambling. In choosing his number or colour, and staking his bet on that choice, the gambler is exercising free will, asserting independence and individuality in a world which, in Greene's novels at least, is depressingly deterministic. Gamblers at Greene's casino are obsessed to the point of desperation with inventing systems, analyzing systems, playing systems, so that Bertram, who gambles away both his money and his marriage, likens them to 'theologians, patiently trying to rationalize a mystery'. As a mathematician, an expert in numbers, Bertram knows that the numerical systems of these 'theologians' will lead nowhere. Bertram's own system is a simple 'faith' in the overall pattern of chance, different from the 'belief' in an invented theory, and one is reminded of the distinction between faith and belief in 'A Visit to Morin'.

In the book's dedication, to A. S. Frere of Heinemann, Greene makes a pointed reference to Catholic interpretations of his novels by saying that he knows Frere, 'unlike some of my Catholic critics', will not confuse the 'I' of the story with its author. It was mainly his reputation as a Catholic writer that Greene needed to escape and in the later books the religious themes are absorbed into the general action, so that although their presence is continually felt, they are no longer dominant.

Comic scenes and characters are scattered throughout all Greene's books, but *Loser Takes All* is his first attempt at a sustained piece of humorous writing. What follows it is a truly comic masterpiece: *Our Man in Havana*. If *Loser Takes All* is amusing, *Our Man in Havana* is hilarious.

As far back as 1936, in a review of Pierre Billou's *Deuxième Bureau*, Greene had played with the idea of a comedy based on the Secret Service: 'What an amusing film of the Secret Service could be made if the intention was satiric and not romantic, the treatment realistic and not violent.' After working for MI6 during the war he had a good deal of first-hand experience of the absurdities of Intelligence. At the request of Alberto Cavalcanti, he planned a film treatment based on an incident he had come across when, working with Kim Philby, he was responsible for counter-intelligence reports from Portugal:

There those Abwehr officers who had not been suborned already by our own service spent much of their time sending home completely erroneous reports based on information received from imaginary agents. It was a paying game, especially when expenses and bonuses were added to the cypher's salary, and a safe one.

The film treatment was never written but the idea remained at the back of Greene's mind, to re-emerge after he had visited Havana several times in the early 1950s. In his original idea, the hero had been cheating the British government in order to support an extravagant wife, but such behaviour would have been seen by the British public not as a joke but, after the war as well as before it, as a heinous crime:

The shadows in 1938 of the war to come had been too dark for comedy; the reader could feel no sympathy for a man who was cheating his country in Hitler's day for the sake of an extravagant wife. But in fantastic Havana, among the absurdities of the Cold War (for who can accept the survival of Western Capitalism as a great cause?) there was a situation allowably comic, all the more if I changed the wife into a daughter.
(*WE*)

At this time the 'extraordinary city' of Havana, 'where every vice was permissible and every trade possible', was ruled over by the tyrannical Batista and it was only after planning his comedy that Greene became aware of the reality of cruelties and injustices under this regime. His novel, however, was concerned not with the local political scene but with the absurdities of the global conflict and the farcical part played in it by the vacuum-cleaner salesman Wormold.

Wormold, who lives in Havana, is recruited as an agent by MI6 and promptly proceeds to exploit and cheat his credulous bosses back in London. He sends them nonsensical reports, which include design plans of a vacuum cleaner purporting to be the design of a secret atomic installation, based on 'information' received from imaginary agents he has 'recruited' – and who are of course in receipt of salaries, bonuses and expenses.

However, the revolutionaries led by Fidel Castro, who were soon to take control, also found the situation 'too dark for comedy' and complained that by making the novel a farce Greene had 'minimized the terror of Batista's rule'. In *The Other Man* Greene defended himself against this charge. He was, he said, 'not in the least sorry' that he had written an 'entertainment' about Cuba rather than a serious novel like *The Quiet American:*

The object was not to talk about Cuba but to make fun of the Secret Service. Havana was merely the background, an accident – it had nothing to do with my sympathy for Fidel.

(Greene's sympathy for Castro is made evident by the fact that since writing *Our Man in Havana* he has visited Cuba, and met Castro, several times and has supported the revolutionary government there in an active and public way: 'Cuba had become . . . one of my commitments.')

Our Man in Havana continues the theme of an innocent at large in the minefield of international politics which was treated in a serious way in *The Quiet American*. Wormold, however, has entirely different motives from Pyle and strays into the minefield almost by accident. The ordinary citizen who becomes involved in the great public world of politics and violence is, as we have seen in the discussion of the 'entertainments', a favourite device of Greene's. So it is that Wormold, like Rowe in *The Ministry of Fear,* suddenly finds his life transformed by melodrama, as if he had entered the world of the thriller writer: 'He stood on the frontier of violence, a strange land he had never visited before.' Here, however, the world of violence is not treated as something mysterious and sinister, but as something frighteningly absurd and chaotic; the world of William Le Queux has been remade by Evelyn Waugh as *Our Man in Havana* becomes a satire not only of the Secret Service but of the now nostalgic melodrama of Greene's own early thrillers. Perhaps the main reason for this difference in tone is that the thrillers were written under the shadow of war, in an atmosphere of violence and expectant fear, whereas after the actual experience of war had been faced, Greene found himself treating essentially the same subjects humorously, 'as though the proximity of death provoked this irresistible urge to laugh and "unwind" ' (*OM*).

The essential subject of the thrillers and *Our Man in Havana* is the conflict between the private individual and the public world of organized power, the 'Kingdoms, republics, powers' which, Wormold's friend Hasselbacher says, 'don't deserve the truth'. As in *The Ministry of Fear* the individual decides to strike back, but what at first seems a harmless joke at the expense, literally, of the Secret Service – creating imaginary but highly profitable

agents and reports – rebounds disturbingly on Wormold as
Hasselbacher and real people with the same names as his 'characters' are assassinated by an unknown power, and an attempt is
made on his own life. As was the case with Pyle, Wormold
becomes 'involved' without pausing to think of the consequences
of his actions, but unlike Pyle he suffers when he realizes the
harm he has caused to others not involved, when he realizes
'There was always another side to a joke, the side of the victim.'
Then, like Fowler, Wormold reluctantly assumes the role of
defender of the individual, the ordinary man, against ideology
and power. He is forced to take the law into his own hands,
seeking not only revenge but justice, and his pursuit of the
mysterious agent Carter, who is responsible for the murder of
Hasselbacher and the others, is an interlude of comparatively
straight thriller writing. In a passage which is central to the whole
meaning of the novel Wormold establishes his motives for killing
Carter:

Wormold said to himself, At least if I could kill him, I would kill for a
clean reason. I would kill to show that you can't kill without being killed
in your turn. I wouldn't kill for my country. I wouldn't kill for capitalism
or Communism or social democracy or the welfare state – whose welfare?
I would kill Carter because he killed Hasselbacher. A family feud had
been a better reason for murder than patriotism or the preference for
one economic system over another. If I love or if I hate, let me love or
hate as an individual. I will not be 59200/5 in anyone's global war.

Confronted with Carter, however, Wormold, with gun in hand,
finds he cannot be one of the inhuman 'judges' who are capable
of deciding that a man must die to further a cause; he sees Carter
no longer as one of the 'private soldiers' but as an individual,
becoming more real and human with every word he says (and the
'excuses' he makes take us back to the extenuating circumstances
of wickedness in Raven and Pinkie):

I have to do it, Wormold thought, before he confesses any more to me.
With every second the man was becoming human, a creature like oneself
whom one might pity or console, not kill. Who knew what excuses were
buried below any violent act?

This being comedy, however, the author allows Wormold to kill Carter in self-defence, thus sparing him the agony of a more cold-blooded execution.

Beatrice, Wormold's secretary, with whom he falls in love, also reaffirms the importance of the individual over countries, and the supremacy of love over ideology. She doesn't 'care a damn about men who are loyal to the people who pay them, to organizations . . .' Back in London she says to Wormold: 'I can't believe in anything bigger than a home, or anything vaguer than a human being.'

Linked with this theme is another: the need to break out of the monotony of being sensible, the need to dream and be 'crazy' and thus affirm individuality. Hasselbacher tells Wormold, 'You should dream more', and when Wormold finally does break out, realizing the absurdity of 'the game' and deciding it was no good playing it 'with half a heart', he is described as 'joyful' – and indeed he is the first joyful figure to appear in Greene's fiction. A song haunts him throughout the story and its refrain becomes an important leitmotif:

> They say the earth is round -
> My madness offends.

Wormold allows his irresponsible side to take over; he gives in to his feelings and his fantasies and this produces a sort of creative madness. He suddenly understands after many years why his daughter Milly had set fire to Thomas Earl Parkman, Jr: 'What a great sense of release you must have experienced . . .' By his creative madness Wormold effectively neutralizes the destructive madness of Hawthorne and his colleagues back in MI6, who, credulous as children, swallow 'nightmares' instead of fairy stories. His madness also wins him Beatrice's love (she is 'deadly bored' with sense). However, the ending of the book, with Wormold getting the OBE for his 'services' and their decision to marry, is not unreservedly happy. There is one doubt in Beatrice's mind: 'she realised the chief problem of this future – that he would never be quite mad enough.'

Our Man in Havana is an accomplished and very funny satire on the organized stupidity that plays dangerously with all our lives, and a celebration of the joy and freedom of the imagination. All Greene's work during this restless decade was an attempt to smash the death mask of his reputation and to break 'the pattern in the carpet', and with *Our Man in Havana* and the novel that followed, *A Burnt-Out Case,* which is dealt with in the previous chapter, he finally succeeded in doing this by developing his fine sense of the absurd.

III

The Comedians is the first of a new phase of mature novels which crown Greene's achievement, and the first of his novels to merge his religious and political preoccupations into a single theme.

The novel opens with a prologue on board the *Medea,* a ship bringing the four central characters – Mr and Mrs Smith, Mr Brown and Major Jones – from the United States to Haiti, the poorest country in the Western hemisphere and at that time (the 1960s) ruled over by one of the world's most ruthless dictators: 'Papa Doc' Duvalier. Under his regime there are no human rights; constitutional laws have been suspended; and people live in fear of his secret police, the Tontons Macoute, who with their black sunglasses are a chilling image of mindless brutality in the novel. (In the 1960s Haiti became one of Greene's political 'commitments' and he visited the country several times, witnessing at first hand atrocities committed by the Tontons Macoute.)

The prologue on the *Medea*, the much discussed 'double start' of the novel, introduces the main characters. That these are named Smith, Brown and Jones is of course a bizarre coincidence which is seen in the novel as yet another instance of the essential absurdity of life. On another level the names serve, like the use of initials in *The Confidential Agent* and of titles in *The Power and the Glory*, to delocalize a situation, showing it as not peculiar to a particular time and place, but as universal.

Mr and Mrs Smith are going to Haiti for the first time and have no idea of the horror they will be forced to witness when they get there. They are an innocent but extremely 'committed' American couple with an absurd and passionate belief in vegetarianism. They have come to help solve Haiti's political problems by setting up a vegetarian centre to fight the 'unwholesome passions' and the 'acidity' caused by eating meat, which they believe to be the main source of all society's ills. In the event, their attempts to do good are thwarted by corrupt officialdom. They are offered an open bribe by a minister to use government grants for the vegetarian centre (which, of course, would never actually be built) as a means of enriching both themselves and the minister, and they witness passion of such 'acidity' that their confidence in the ultimate powers of vegetarianism is shaken.

Brown, the narrator, is middle-aged, rootless and, like Fowler in *The Quiet American*, resolutely 'uninvolved' and uncommitted. This lack of commitment he traces back to his rootlessness ('I am from Monaco. . . That is almost the same as being a citizen of nowhere.') and his loss of faith. Now, he explains, he is simply resigned to taking the world as it comes. He is returning to Haiti to look after the Trianon, a hotel in Port-au-Prince which he has inherited from his unconventional, life-loving mother, the 'Countess', and which he has been trying unsuccessfully to sell in New York. He is also returning to a dying love affair with Martha, the wife of a South American ambassador and daughter of a Nazi war criminal.

'Major' Jones is an ex-actor who boasts not only a false military title, but a false record of heroism in the war (he had in fact been rejected by the army for flat feet). He is a con-man whose visit to Haiti is, unlike the Smiths', based entirely on self-interest. He has come to plan an arms deal with officials he knows to be corrupt, but in the volatile world of Haitian politics he is unable to keep up with the changes of political fortunes and when his scheme to swindle the government backfires he is forced to take political asylum with Martha and her husband in the embassy.

When Brown returns to the Trianon at the start of the novel, he finds in the hotel pool the dead body of the ex-Secretary of State for Social Welfare, Dr Philipot. Philipot, having fallen from grace with the President, had decided to commit suicide rather than let himself be taken by the Tontons Macoute. Although Brown is unmoved by Dr Philipot's fate, and by the other evidence of tyranny around him, his association with Smith and Jones, and the Secretary's choice of the Trianon's pool as the place to kill himself, involve him accidentally and reluctantly in the country's politics, and in the end he actively takes sides by supporting a group of revolutionary guerrillas led by Philipot's son. However, his motives in doing this are more personal than ideological: suspecting Jones of seducing Martha, he traps him through his lying boasts about wartime heroics into offering to help the inexperienced guerrillas. So determined is he to call Jones's bluff and to make sure he does what he has promised, that he even escorts Jones in person in his dangerous escape from the embassy to the guerrilla camp in the mountains.

Although the three characters are of equal importance in the story, the events are narrated by Brown and it is through his ironic, pessimistic gaze that we see and interpret the action. To Brown, life is a humourless comedy, with actors and actresses ('comedians') directed by a God who is 'the authorative practical joker', and who drives them 'to the extreme point of comedy' which is often, as in the case of Jones, their death. Brown's view of life permeates the narration, with its repeated use of the language of the theatre, and especially of key words such as 'charades', 'actors', 'parts', and 'tragic themes'. His affair with Martha is described as 'a little sub-plot affording a little light relief', belonging to 'the world of comedy and not of tragedy'. There are references to actual plays (*Hamlet* and *Othello*) and there are even several pieces of direct acting: the ship's concert; the young Brown's dressing up as an adult to gain entrance to the casino; and Jones's disguising himself as a woman to escape from the police.

The 'comedians' of the title are those, like Brown and Jones, who pretend or act and who thus avoid not only their true selves, but any involvement or commitment – and commitment is the novel's central theme. It is because of their commitment that the Smiths are not comedians, despite their eccentricity and essential ridiculousness. Their dedication to 'true vegetarianism' is a pathetic and laughable substitute for real faith, but they are at least sincere in their belief, and for Brown sincerity is proof that someone is not a comedian. The Smiths are heroic, too, as Brown says, with 'a gentle heroism' that stems from their having been born with 'peace in their hearts' rather than the 'splinter of ice'.

Some reviewers claimed that Greene's treatment of the Smiths somehow made up for his anti-Americanism in *The Quiet American.* This is hard to see, for, despite all their good intentions, they are absurd. Besides, strong criticism of United States foreign policy underlies the story, a criticism aimed mainly at U.S. fear of having a Communist state in its 'back yard'. A consequence of this fear is that the State Department sees Papa Doc as 'a bulwark against communism' and is therefore prepared to support him. The main critic of America in the novel is Brown's friend, the highly 'involved' Doctor Magiot, who knows that if there were no Communists, like himself, 'Papa Doc would cease to be a bulwark of the free world.' He tells the Smiths: 'In the western hemisphere, in Haiti and elsewhere, we live under the shadow of your great and prosperous country. Much patience and courage is needed to keep one's head.'

Mr Smith's ridiculous, doomed scheme for a vegetarian centre is itself a comment on Western aid in the Third World, as is his giving money to the cripple in Duvalierville. This last is 'a good action', one that eases his liberal conscience and gives him 'a sense of happiness'; what he does not realize is that the cripple is immediately robbed by the figure of corrupt officialdom, the justice of the peace. Eventually Smith is disillusioned by the corruption of the officials and distributes his 'aid' by throwing money to the beggars outside the Post Office, a final act of hopelessness which produces a wild, ruthless scramble: 'Men with two legs kicked down men with one, men with two arms grasped those who were armless by their torsos and threw them to the ground.'

Brown is, as mentioned above, similar to Fowler in *The Quiet American:* the 'uncommitted' hero who reluctantly and with ambiguous personal motives becomes involved in politics, taking the side of the oppressed. Brown's motives, however, are clearly more selfish than Fowler's. Fowler at least expresses a deep concern in the end for the injustice and suffering he sees around him, but Brown's sole impulse is jealousy. Like Querry in *A Burnt-Out Case,* he has 'lost completely the capacity to be concerned'; 'somewhere years ago' he had 'forgotten how to be involved in anything'. After visiting Jones in prison Brown warns Mr Smith: 'I wonder if we ought to involve ourselves any further.' Smith replies, 'We are involved', and Brown realizes that the vegetarian 'was thinking in the big terms I could not recognize, like Mankind, Justice, The Pursuit of Happiness'.

Brown's spiritual and moral incapacities are due, like Querry's, to a loss of faith, and as with Querry the loss of faith in God has meant a total loss of any faith, of the ability to believe in anything. At the end Doctor Magiot pleads with him, 'If you have abandoned one faith, do not abandon all faith.' There is, says Magiot, always an alternative faith, whether Marxism, in his own case, or the pagan voodooism of the oppressed and fearful Haitians, or that travesty of real faith, the Smiths' obsession with vegetarianism. Magiot wonders whether these alternatives are not perhaps just 'the same faith under another mask', but for Brown it is too late, he has lost all faith and is resigned to 'take things as they come', which is 'what most of the world does, surely?'

Martha is also not involved: 'Action is dangerous, isn't it?' she asks Brown, reflecting on the fate of her German father who had become involved and who was consequently tried as a war criminal. The Resistance medal found among the effects of Brown's mother after her death suggests to him that 'she must have gone into the streets too'. But what the children have learned from their parents' 'example' is to try to lead their own private lives, unconcerned by what is going on around them. Even so, though Brown and Martha have no beliefs or convictions, they cannot remain apart from the world, a fact that is most clearly brought home in their moments of love-making, when the world intrudes upon their privacy. First, Brown is reminded of Philipot's dead body and is rendered impotent by the thought:

She had drawn up her knees and I was reminded of Doctor Philipot's body under the diving board: birth, love and death in their positions closely resemble each other. I found I could do nothing. . .

Later, as they lie in bed together at the Trianon, the sound of shots breaks in on their intimacy: prisoners are being executed as a reprisal for an attack on the police station. Brown's only reaction this time is to say '. . . you'd better wait for the audience to disperse', but the noise of the execution leads them to talk again of Martha's father. He is a significant figure in the story because he serves to show that Haiti is not an isolated example of tyranny and violence, 'not an exception in a sane world', but 'a small slice of everything taken at random'. He also serves to introduce the theme that it is better to be committed, though wrong, than to be uncommitted, when, at another moment of intimacy, his ghost and Philipot's corpse again come between Brown and Martha:

'And people in Germany too cut their throats to escape his [Martha's father's] justice.'
'Yes. The situation isn't abnormal. It belongs to human life. Cruelty's like a searchlight. It sweeps from one spot to another. We only escape it from a time. We are trying to hide now under the palm trees.'
'Instead of doing anything?'
'Instead of doing anything.'
She said, 'I almost prefer my father.'

This has echoes of the T. S. Eliot quotation cited in Chapter Four, that 'it is better, in a paradoxical way, to do evil than to do nothing: at least we exist.' Here it is doing nothing which itself is seen as evil, not just by Doctor Magiot, but more significantly by a refugee Haitian priest who delivers a liberationist sermon to the survivors in Santo Domingo. The priest appears, as at the end of so many of Greene's novels, almost as a chorus, not to restore the teachings of the Church, but to provide a sense of perspective and to underline the main issues of the story. He is a liberationist, part of the originally South American movement of Liberation Theology which links the teachings of the gospel with political involvement – described here in *A Theology of Liberation* by Gustavo Gutierrez:

The annunciation of the Gospel thus has a conscientizing function, or in other words, a politicizing function . . . But this is made real and meaningful only by living and announcing the Gospel from within a commitment to liberation, only in concrete, effective solidarity with people and exploited social classes.

Christ's message, according to liberationists, is political and social as well as spiritual, intended to disturb the powerful and give hope to the powerless. Greene claimed in *The Other Man* that *The Comedians* is the only book he has written from a specific political point of view and 'in order to fight – to fight the horror of Papa Doc's dictatorship'. It is significant then that in this, his most overtly political novel, he merges the political with the religious for the first time and for the first time portrays a priest who is in any way adequate to the situation, who is able to give an answer, albeit an unorthodox one, to the people who come to him with their sufferings. The priest condemns the indifference of people like Brown, an indifference that is 'the perfection of egoism', and advocates instead political militancy. Thus the Church is seen to be rediscovering 'the technique of revolution' Greene had found missing in Mexico in 1938 (see page 80) and is seen for the first time in the novels as a possible source of strength. However, it is a strength which resorts to fighting violence with violence, and which is theologically 'wrong', in the words of the priest:

'. . . The Church condemns violence, but it condemns indifference more harshly. Violence can be the expression of love, indifference never. One is an imperfection of charity, the other the perfection of egoism. In the days of fear, doubt and confusion, the simplicity and loyalty of one apostle advocated a political solution. He was wrong, but I would rather be wrong with St Thomas than right with the cold and the craven . . .'

It is in this condemnation of indifference and support of the oppressed against the oppressor that Catholic and Communist can now meet, and the last word is given to the Communist, Doctor Magiot, as Brown reads his final letter:

Catholics and Communists have committed great crimes, but at least they have not stood aside, like an established society, and been indifferent. I would rather have blood on my hands than water like Pilate.

IV

The humour of *The Comedians* has a pessimistic note: the grim irony and absurdity of life as observed by Brown; the 'humour of the defeated' in the British Consul; and the journalist Petit

Pierre's 'gaiety of despair'. Life is a bad joke at our expense, and there are 'only two possible attitudes', misery or gaiety, but the laughter has a hollow ring to it. In the next book, however, the pendulum swings back to the manic side of Greene's manic-depressive personality, and there is no shadow cast over the humour in *Travels with My Aunt*. This is the only book, according to Greene, that he has written solely 'for the fun of it'. He himself has a high opinion of it, but many British critics have objected to the book's loosely constructed, anecdotal nature. In *The Other Man* Greene gave an account of the genesis of the novel:

I'd embarked on this adventure for my own amusement, with no notion of what might happen the next day. A number of ideas I expected to use in short stories became recollections of old Augusta. I was surprised that they all cohered into a logical sequence, and that the novel became a finished product, for I'd been regarding it more as an exercise based on the free association of ideas . . .

The story is a simple one: Henry Pulling, as he begins retire-ment and old age, is liberated at the eleventh hour, so to speak, from a lifetime of conventionality and boredom by his outra-geous, life-loving septuagenarian aunt. In the rough process of liberation Henry discovers not only that she is his true mother, but that her lifestyle, of which he had at first disapproved, is at least preferable to the empty, bland respectability of his own life as a provincial bank manager. Their adventures together also enable Aunt Augusta to tell Henry her life story, and thus a series of vignettes in the present are interspersed with a series of vignettes from the past, giving the effect of a rather loosely arranged picaresque.

Greene's comic powers here reach their peak, as the vivid, somewhat grotesque characters of Henry and Augusta represent two opposing attitudes to life in a truly hilarious dialogue. Augusta's tireless pursuit of love and amusement, and her determined 'liberation' of Henry constitute a celebration of individualism, as opposed to dull conformity, and of vitality, laughter, and the power of imagination to transform life.

Greene begins Henry and Augusta's travels by retracing some of the steps he had taken in earlier novels – to Brighton, to the East on the Orient Express – and he also brings into use again some of his favourite conventions. Henry is one of a long line of 'reluctant heroes' who get dragged into an experience of the hostile, adult world, whether it is the world of politics, violence, or, as in Henry's case, the world of sexuality and law breaking, though the 'criminality' he encounters – the possession of marijuana, currency and tobacco smuggling, confidence trickery – is of an innocent kind compared to the violence and murder of Greene's earlier criminals. Henry differs from other reluctant characters also in that he gradually begins to *enjoy* the incursion of this outside world on his own. This is because he is also in the mould of another of Greene's regular characters, the middle-aged or old man making a burst for freedom, like Wormold, Monsignor Quixote and indeed Greene himself (see page 102), who attributes the manic mood of the novel to a sense of liberation in his own private life:

I can only suppose it came from making a difficult decision in my private life and leaving England to settle permanently in France in 1966. I burned a number of boats and in the light of the flames I began again to write a novel.
(*WE*)

When he is first caught up in Augusta's world Henry feels 'a sense of fear and exhilaration', and when, in the middle of the novel, he temporarily parts from Augusta and resumes his carefully arranged life of quiet retirement, he realizes the emptiness and meaninglessness of that life. At this moment he changes from an innocent reluctantly caught up in a strange world to a captive wanting to make a bid for freedom. The change comes as soon as he lets himself back into the empty house:

I was afraid of burglars and Indian thugs and snakes and fires and Jack the Ripper, when I should have been afraid of thirty years in a bank and a take-over bid and a premature retirement and the Deuil du Roy Albert [one of the dahlias which constitute his hobby].

Through his aunt Henry sees his past life as a prison and through her he frees himself from it and from his negative sense of morality. He experiences in this liberation a feeling of elation merely at being alive, the sort of elation felt by Wormold in *Our Man in Havana*.

There is in Augusta a strong echo of Brown's mother in *The Comedians*. Both women have dubious claims to the title of Countess; both have a colourful history of romance and adventure; their current lovers are both young negroes who die, and Augusta could be said to have, like Brown's mother, 'an easy enlightened eighteenth-century air'. Augusta is a life-giving force, devoted to the pursuit of love and fun. She is disreputable, with a total disregard for the restrictive bourgeois morality which Henry represents, yet by the end he realizes 'there seemed nothing so very wrong in her *curriculum vitae,* nothing so wrong as thirty years in a bank.' Her morality is simply an expression of her own dynamic, anarchic approach to life and as Henry is engulfed by her he discovers for the first time with a sense of pride that he too has 'a streak of anarchy'. She believes in nothing except the power of love and the need to go on living as long as she can, yet her attitude to life is seen as more compassionate, more full of humanity than the attitude represented by Henry, as when she turns on him with a flash of anger:

'I despise no one,' she said, 'no one. Regret your own actions, if you like that kind of wallowing in self-pity, but never, never despise. Never presume yours is a better morality . . . But you, I suppose, never cheated in all your little provincial banker's life because there's not anything you wanted enough, not even money, not even a woman.'

In *The End of the Affair,* Bendrix compares life to a novel, with God the novelist having total control over characters and plot; in *Our Man in Havana,* however, Wormold, who talks and thinks 'like a novelist', tries to take the plot into his own hands and, to a certain extent, succeeds. In *Travels with My Aunt,* Augusta, too, takes the plot into her own hands, and takes control over her own destiny. Indeed Henry sees her as a creative writer inventing both her own world and the people in it, and considers himself as the reader of this life/novel. As he listens to Augusta's stories he feels as though he 'had borrowed my aunt's vision':

I thought of Curran and Mr Visconti – they lived in my imagination as though she had actually created them . . . Perhaps if she ever talked about me to another – I could well imagine what a story she could make out of my dahlias and my silly tenderness for Tooley and my stainless past – even I would come to some sort of life, and the character she drew, I felt sure, would be much more vivid than the real I.

Greene is fascinated by the relationship between fiction, man's invented world, and the 'real' world we live in; by the way we invent characters in our own lives; and by the way life can sometimes seem to imitate fiction. He comments on *Travels with My Aunt:*

Some critics have found in the book a kind of resumé of my literary career – a scene in Brighton, the journey on the Orient Express, and perhaps a hint of this did come to my mind by the time Aunt Augusta arrived at the Pera Palace, but what struck me with some uneasiness, when I reread the book the other day, were the suggestions I found in it of where the future was going to take me [that is, to the town of Corrientes in northern Argentina where he found the setting for *The Honorary Consul*].
(*WE*)

On a more ordinary as well as a more serious level, in *Travels with My Aunt* Henry realizes how life imitates art when he writes, 'One's life is more formed, I sometimes think, by books than by human beings.' The lack of love in his own life, he concludes, is perhaps because his father's library 'had not contained the right books'. That this echoes Greene's own feelings is made evident by one of the several small private 'jokes' (the self-references and the use of real names) in the novel: in his essay 'The Lost Childhood', Greene had explained the enormous influence Marjorie Bowen's *Viper of Milan* had had on him as a child – giving him both the will to write and the theme about which to write – and Augusta's lover Visconti takes his name from Greene's favourite character in that book. In *Ways of Escape* Greene described how it gave him 'an innocent amusement' to hear Detective John Sparrow (named after the celebrated ex-warden of All Souls) describe Visconti as 'a viper'. A full circle is reached when the writer, whose 'pattern' has been derived from such fictional characters as Visconti, is in turn influenced by the fictional characters he creates himself, as Greene declares he is in *The Other Man*: 'The fact is, one is changed by one's books. The writer plays God until his creatures escape from him and, in their turn, they mould him.'

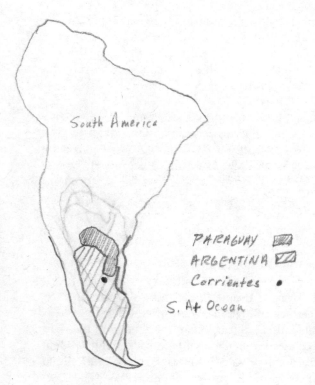

7 Absurdity and Hope

I

'Politics are in the air we breathe, like the presence or absence of a God', Greene declared in *The Other Man*. The statement could serve as an epigraph for *The Honorary Consul*, in which belief in God inevitably involves the believer in questions about where he stands in politics. *The Honorary Consul* is, like *The Comedians*, mainly about commitment. In it, as in the earlier novel, Greene combines various forms of commitment – political, religious and emotional – into a single, seamless theme. This fusion is highlighted by Greene's choice of epigraph, from Thomas Hardy: 'All things merge in one another – good into evil, generosity into justice, religion into politics . . .'

The novel is set in Corrientes, a small town in northern Argentina, near the border with Paraguay. Again as in *The Comedians*, the action revolves around three main characters: Dr Eduardo Plarr, Father León Rivas, and Charley Fortnum, the Honorary British Consul. Plarr, a middle-aged doctor, is 'indifferent', like Greene's earlier heroes Querry, Fowler and Brown. He is a burnt-out case incapable of any form of commitment, whether political, religious or emotional. Like Fowler and Brown, however, he becomes reluctantly involved, by helping an amateurish group of Paraguayan Marxist freedom fighters in their attempt to kidnap the American Ambassador to Argentina. Plarr's motives for helping them are mainly personal: the group is led by his old schoolfriend, León Rivas, a liberationist priest who has sided with the poor and oppressed to the extent that he has taken up arms in the struggle for their liberation; also, the freedom of Plarr's English father, a political prisoner in Paraguay, is part of the exchange deal demanded by the kidnappers (though this is a trick on Plarr, for the kidnappers know that his father is in fact dead).

In the event, the inept guerrillas bungle the kidnap attempt and seize by mistake the Honorary Consul, Charley Fortnum. He is without any political importance, being more of an embarrassment than an asset to the Diplomatic Service. He is an alcoholic *mate* farmer who has recently found a new reason for living in his love for Clara, a girl from the local brothel whom he has married despite the scandal but who is, unknown to him, Plarr's mistress and pregnant by him. In the end both Plarr and Fortnum are trapped in a hut with the guerrillas, who refuse to believe what is in fact the truth, that the British Government will gladly sacrifice Fortnum in order to make a show of firmness in not giving in to terrorists. The kidnappers announce their intention of killing Fortnum if their demands are not met, but before then the police discover the hideout and rescue Fortnum, killing in the process Plarr, Rivas, Aquino and the other guerrillas – all of whom, and especially Rivas, are good men treated with sympathy by Greene.

Such a brief outline of the plot cannot convey the structural richness of this, Greene's most subtle, complex and accomplished novel, nor the depth and range of its characters. The events do not change the characters, as in Greene's earlier novels (particularly those, like *The Man Within* and *It's a Battlefield,* most influenced by Conrad), but reveal and release their true potential: the latent courage in the cowardly Charley Fortnum as he faces death, and the latent capacity for love in the 'indifferent' Plarr and Clara.

At the beginning of the novel Plarr is a 'cold fish' deliberately avoiding love, just as he avoids politics. Both love and politics are for him a form of involvement or commitment, with responsibilities he is not prepared to accept: ' "Love" was a claim which he wouldn't meet, a responsibility he would refuse to accept, a demand . . .' We are told that Plarr 'felt no belief in sexual love' and, elsewhere, that he was suspicious 'of any emotion which was curable by means as simple as an orgasm or an éclair'. The 'éclair' refers to his mother's dramatized weeping when parted from her husband, a distress forgotten in time as she gratifies herself with cream cakes. Plarr's refusal to accept the responsibilities of love is traced back to his mother's emotional blackmail

('Put up your hands or else . . .') while he feels that he had perhaps 'loved his father all the more because he had never used the word ['love'] or asked for anything'.

Clara is also emotionally 'burnt-out' and incapable of love after her time in Mother Sanchez's brothel. The emotional mutilation she has suffered there is symbolized by her skilful pretence of enjoying sex (though she in fact feels nothing) – for she knows this pleases the 'customer', even when it is Charley Fortnum or Eduardo Plarr. However, when she is with Plarr, who demands that she give up the pretence, she experiences sexual pleasure for the first time, which she interprets as a sign of her genuine love for him. But, knowing his hostility to emotional involvement she again acts, this time to hide her enjoyment:

She said, 'Do you remember that time at the camp when I told you I was pretending? But, *caro,* I was not pretending. Now when you make love to me I pretend. I pretend I feel nothing. I bite my lip so as to pretend. Is it because I love you, Eduardo? Do you think I love you?'

Plarr does not answer the question, but from that moment, we are told, 'he began to feel guilt for his egoism' – a guilt which is his first step towards a form of 'recovery', to use the terms of *A Burnt-Out Case*. For the first time he recognizes the importance of emotional commitment, and says to Fortnum, who has just learned of his affair with Clara: ' "It's not as if she or I really cared for each other. Caring is the only dangerous thing, Fortnum." '

Fortnum on the other hand, for all his absurdity, truly loves Clara, and capacity to love is 'the great test', the criterion by which both believers and non-believers are judged in Greene's novels. Plarr in the end is 'jealous' not of Fortnum's role as husband to Clara, but of his very ability to love her, a love of which he himself is incapable:

'I'm jealous because he loves her. That stupid banal word love. It's never meant anything to me. Like the word God. I know how to fuck – I don't know how to love. Poor drunken Charley Fortnum wins the game.'

Plarr's jealousy is, as Fortnum is aware, evidence that he has actually begun to love Clara 'in his way', for jealousy is at least an emotion, where Plarr previously was entirely without feeling. At the same time as Plarr admits his jealousy, he also decides to try to negotiate with the police surrounding the hut in an attempt to save not just Fortnum's life, but the lives of León and his group. However, this act of bravery results in his own death, as the paratroopers shoot him down before he has even had a chance to talk. His death resembles the machismo deaths of much South American literature: a brave man walking out alone to face his death, shot down and left to die in the dirt. Aquino, one of the terrorists, gibes at him for this display of machismo, but Plarr tells him, 'It's not machismo I'm suffering from.' His decision to leave the hut is a form of genuine courage, and is evidence that with his emotional 'recovery' he has at the same time become truly 'involved', and accepted the individual's responsibility for moral action.

Fortnum is the only one in the hut to survive the police action and he returns to Clara knowing that she has betrayed his love and that the child in her womb is not his. However, it is not this which turns him against her, but her own apparent 'indifference' to Plarr's death, her own inability to love. Plarr, he reflects bitterly, 'had not earned a single tear', and as Clara goes to kiss him he draws away, for 'A kiss was worth nothing from someone who was incapable of loving even her lover.' But Clara's indifference is only pretence and finally she does give in to her feelings and breaks into tears. Paradoxically, it is at this moment, when she cries for her dead lover, that Fortnum feels closest to her, for it shows him that she is after all capable of love and is not 'all deception'. Fortnum then tries to convince her that Plarr really had begun to love her. He also acknowledges his own, ironically 'fatherly' love for him, and suggests they name the child after him. It is Greene's most optimistic ending.

Fortnum emerges from his ordeal as a character of considerable courage and compassion. While being held by the terrorists he dictates what he expects to be his last message to Clara, for his death at the hands of León Rivas now seems inevitable. In the letter he tells Clara that before he knew her he was 'a finished man', with nothing to look forward to except the next drink. But then he found her and with her a new life, 'something I really wanted to do'. His love for Clara and the expected child, his desire to protect them and make them happy, thus fills the void of an otherwise meaningless existence. His subsequent abduction by the revolutionaries then threatens to deprive him of all this, as it takes him to 'the anteroom of death'. However, although he has always seen himself as a coward since childhood, his calm acceptance of what he believes to be inevitable death reveals a true courage. Also, as he faces death his compassion for others increases. He feels 'an odd kinship' with his 'murderer', Father Rivas, who is 'a good man', and he actually tries to comfort the priest and make his job easier: 'Does a condemned man always have to comfort his executioner?' he wonders, while asking, 'Is there anything I can do for you, Father?' Fortnum even thinks that at one point the priest is going to confess to him, 'And by God I'd have given him absolution.'

Fortnum's attitude to Plarr and Clara also changes as the 'final hour' approaches and he thinks that at least Plarr will survive to take care of her and the baby. He then tears up the sentimental letter he has written ('Why should she care to hear a lot of loving from me if she has you?') and says: 'Promise you won't tell her that I knew about you. I wouldn't want her to feel any guilt. If she's capable of it.'

Fortnum even reconciles himself to the memory of his father (his hatred of whom he now realizes 'was only one of my mistakes') as his mind goes back to the traumatic moment of his childhood when, having fallen off a horse at the age of six, his father, too drunk even to recognize him, had looked on helplessly:

He had a vision of his father sitting bewildered, not understanding, not recognizing him, by the dumb-waiter, while he lay on the ground and the horse stood over him. Poor bugger, he thought.

Father Rivas's ending is optimistic too, though in a more paradoxical way. As leader of a band of idealistic but inept revolutionaries his plans go horribly wrong, for instead of saving the lives of ten men (the Paraguayan political prisoners) as intended, he finds himself in the position of having to murder one ('I never believed I would have to take a life'). At the end, however, he runs out of the hut to comfort the dying Plarr and is himself shot, before he has time to kill Fortnum. The police and the powers of tyranny have won, but his death is in one way a

triumph for it has saved him from mortal sin. When both he and
Plarr are lying wounded, he whispers that he is safe, now. 'Safe?'
asks Plarr:

> 'Quite safe. I could not kill a mouse.' Doctor Plarr said, 'We must get
> you to a hospital.'
> 'You were right, Eduardo,' the voice said. 'I was never made to be a
> killer.'

It is a credit to Greene's powers of characterization, however,
that throughout the ordeal the reader could not doubt that,
although profoundly reluctant to do so, Rivas was completely
capable of murdering Fortnum if necessary.

As we have seen, at the end of *The Comedians* a Haitian priest
gives a liberationist sermon in which he declares that, for a
Christian, violence in pursuit of justice is preferable to indifference in the face of injustice. The ethical problem of violence as a
political means to a Christian end is at the centre of *The Honorary
Consul,* in which trouble in 'a quiet province', subdued by poverty
and tyranny, is caused by 'one of those third world priests' who in
this case literally takes up arms himself. Here Greene is back in
the realm of 'situation ethics' which he had earlier explored in his
'Catholic novels'. In the character of a revolutionary priest he
finds great scope for exploring moral ambiguity and paradox:
Rivas is the good man condemned by the Church, forced into
mortal sin to work for a Christian end.

It is interesting to compare Rivas with an earlier Greene priest
who was also unable to keep the rules of the Church – the whisky
priest in *The Power and the Glory* – for there are certain similari-
ties between them and significant differences. Both move from
being the priest of the rich to being the priest of the poor, and
although Rivas's Church has altered radically, it is still a Church
in which the archbishop can sit down at the general's table with a
clear conscience and in which the curia can keep their hands
clean of involvement, like Pilate. Both priests possess a social
conscience and a strong sense of compassion for the suffering of
others, but their difference lies in their solutions to the problem.
The whisky priest does not believe in political struggle, for the
spiritual problems of the poor would not be solved by their
becoming rich. He believes instead that only in the power of

prayer and God's mercy in answering that prayer is there hope. For Rivas, however, the political and spiritual are inseparable parts of the human situation and this leads him to an extreme form of non-conformity. Not only do the teachings of the Church seem to him inadequate to cope with man's current historical situation, but the teachings of Christ, too:

Some of the rules He laid down were only the rules of a good man. A man who lived in his own province, in his own particular day. He had no idea of the kind of world we would be living in now. Render unto Caesar, but when *our* Caesar uses Napalm and fragmentation bombs . . . The Church lives in time too.

But, he goes on to say, the memory of Christ can lift people out of 'the temporary Church' – the Church of the archbishop and his priest who refuse to attend to the dying in the *barrio* – into the 'great Church' beyond time and place.

Rivas thus loses faith in the Church but not in God, and the Mass said in his wet shirt, with just bread and wine and a few candles, is a sign (as it was in *The Power and the Glory* and is in the later *Monsignor Quixote*) of the strength of the priest's belief and a demonstration that the sacraments do not depend on the correct canonical paraphernalia, or even on the Church, for their power.

As he lies dying, Rivas begins an act of contrition and Plarr jokes, *'Ego te absolvo.'* The joke falls flat even for him, however. The laugh 'shrivels in his throat' and it is suggested that Rivas is absolved: even Fortnum swore that if he had the power he would have absolved him. Despite the official condemnation of Rivas after his death, he is not the merciless 'fanatical priest' the novelist Saavedra calls him, but the 'good man' Fortnum acknowledges him to have been.

When trying to persuade Fortnum to make a last confession, Father Rivas in a way makes his own confession:

'There is one thing I can easily say. Perhaps you could say it too. I am sorry not to have had more patience. Failures like ours are often just failures of hope. Please – cannot you say you are sorry you did not have more hope?'

The man obviously needed comfort and Charley Fortnum gave him all he could. 'Yes, I suppose I could go about as far as that, Father.'

Loss of hope is the failure of many of Greene's characters. Here, however, despite the despair, there is hope in the survival of love, in the feeling of closeness to Clara that Fortnum experiences at the end; there is hope too in the absolution of Rivas, even in the survival of the truth about what happened, despite the official lies, and in Fortnum's commitment to that truth.

The position of the believer is also shown as more hopeful, in Rivas's speculation about the evolution of God into a wholly good God, through the good works of man on earth. Rivas holds God responsible for the evil in the world as well as the good, and sees Him as having a 'night-time face' as well as a 'day-time face'. Like Dr Colin in *A Burnt-Out Case,* he seems to have read Teilhard de Chardin, for he believes in man's spiritual evolution and through that to God's evolution towards the perfection of goodness in Christ:

'Because the evolution of God depends on our evolution. Every evil act of ours strengthens His night-side, and every good one helps His day-side. We belong to Him and He belongs to us. But now at least we can be sure where evolution will end one day – it will end in a goodness like Christ's. It is a terrible process all the same and the God I believe in suffers as we suffer while He struggles against Himself – against His evil side.'

Plarr, on the other hand, finds no comfort in God. He does not believe in Him, except as evil, as 'that horror up there sitting in the clouds'. He sees no evidence around him of Rivas's God, and tends the sick as well as he can because 'he can't leave that to God', just as Rivas is forced to take up arms himself because he has 'never yet seen any sign that He interferes in our wars or our politics'. As in *The Comedians* God is seen again as the great practical joker, and life is absurd. We all get 'caught up' in it, as we get caught up in love, 'by mistake'. We are all reluctant heroes. 'Life is absurd' is the message of all the novels since *A Burnt-Out Case,* but it is reiterated here with a new note of optimism, even from the non-believer, Plarr: 'Nothing is ineluctable. Life has surprises. Life is absurd. Because it's absurd there is always hope.'

II

After finishing *The Comedians* Greene began writing *The Human Factor,* the story of a British double agent, Maurice Castle, who leaks classified information to the Soviet Union. Greene abandoned the novel, however, for it was seemingly 'anticipated' by the notorious, real-life Philby affair. While in the Secret Service during the war Greene had known and worked with Kim Philby, the most famous of all British double agents, and he disliked the idea of the novel being taken as a *roman à clef.* However, the book continued to 'nag' at Greene's memory and after the publication of *The Honorary Consul* he 'reluctantly and doubtfully' resumed work on the manuscript.

After his experience of Intelligence work, which contained 'little excitement or melodrama', Greene planned to write an espionage novel which was more realistic than romantic, and which was 'free from the conventional violence, which has not, in spite of James Bond, been a feature of the British Secret Service':

I wanted to present the Service unromantically as a way of life, men going daily to their office to earn their pensions, the background much like that of any other profession – whether the bank clerk or the business director – an undangerous routine, and within each character the more important private life.
(*WE*)

Back in the 1930s Greene had learned from Buchan 'the enormous dramatic value of adventure in familiar surroundings happening to unadventurous men' ('The Last Buchan'). This intrusion of adventure on normality is the convention on which all Greene's thrillers are based – including *The Human Factor,* in which spies are dull commuters, unhappy, ageing divorcees, middle-class bureaucrats, or careerists without ideals. Greene's portrayal of day-to-day espionage in the office scenes, between dull, contented Castle and his restless, bored colleague Davis, is one of unglamorous and tedious routine.

On the surface *The Human Factor* uses many of the conventions of the modern spy novel. There is the usual Intelligence jargon of 'traces', 'drops', and references to the Chief of Security as 'C'.

High-powered decision-making takes place in the dining rooms
of gentlemens' clubs, while those at the top firmly adhere to their
public school backgrounds and maintain an atmosphere of cult-
ural snobbery in the corridors of power. But just as Greene's
thrillers of the 1930s extended the genre to accommodate a more
serious moral purpose, so his spy story of the 1970s has a deeper
concern with the 'human factor' behind the action than the
standard Cold War espionage thriller exemplified by such writers
as Len Deighton and John Le Carré – writers who have in fact
been influenced by Greene's own early thrillers. *The Human
Factor* is about the people who happen to be spies rather than
about spying *per se*.

A security leak is discovered in a small sub-section of SIS
dealing with African affairs. Of the two 'suspects', Maurice Castle
is ruled out by Doctor Percival, the sinister and ruthless senior
officer in charge of the investigation, because although 'brilliant
with files', Castle is too dull a man to be a double agent, and too
close to retirement. Castle's young colleague Davis, on the other
hand, seems to be a classic suspect: intelligent, restless, and with
a life style seemingly beyond his income. On the basis of little
more than a hunch, Percival concludes that Davis is the mole and
decides, almost unilaterally, that yet another security scandal
would be unacceptably damaging to the Service and that therefore
Davis should be quietly eliminated. Davis, however, is entirely
innocent and it is Castle who has been feeding classified information tö the Soviets over a number of years. He has done this not
out of any ideological support for the Soviet system, but because
his black South African wife Sarah, and her young son Sam, were
both aided in their escape from the South African security forces
by a Communist friend, and Castle's only means of repaying the
debt of gratitude he owed him was by passing information to his
Russian masters.

After Davis is murdered, and after Castle has fallen into a trap
set by Percival, Castle realizes he has been discovered and escapes
to Moscow with the help of the KGB and of Halliday, a Communist bookshop owner who has been Castle's contact in the field.
In making his escape Castle is forced to leave behind Sarah and
Sam, on the understanding that they will follow on afterwards.
But they are refused passports by a vengeful Home Office and so

Castle faces the prospect of a lonely and empty old age exiled in his Moscow apartment.

The political background of the story is sketched in with consummate skill. The British Secret Service is collaborating with the South African government on Operation Uncle Remus, an appalling 'Final Solution' to South Africa's racial problems. This has a disturbing air of reality about it, and Greene considers it 'less an invention than a prediction'.

This background of *realpolitik* does much to make the rest of the story convincing, though unfortunately the reader's credibility is severely strained by certain implausible turns of plot at key moments. Take, for example, Castle's great ineptitude during his escape, agreeing to meet the American agent Blit for a Planter's Punch 'in half an hour', when one imagines that a trained field agent, as Castle is, would have been able to extricate himself from the unexpected encounter with a suitable excuse. Similarly, the Soviet Intelligence officer responsible for Castle's escape chooses to disguise him as a blind man – a disguise which would demand considerable acting skills from a man in an extreme state of nervous tension. Especially unconvincing is Doctor Percival's one-man decision to eliminate Davis on the flimsiest of circumstantial evidence. When Kim Philby read the book in Moscow he thought the ruthless Percival an unlikely member of the British Secret Service and suggested, 'with justice' according to Greene, that he must have been recruited from the CIA.

Greene had intended the novel to be free of 'conventional violence', but Percival's cold-blooded murder of Davis and Castle's having to kill the family dog, Buller, in order not to be given away by his barking, do in fact introduce a note of violence and melodrama, as Greene acknowledged:

I had betrayed my purpose. There *was* violence . . . It wasn't as realistic a picture as I had intended, and the novel was saved only by the human factor of the title. As a love story – a married-love story of an elderly man – I think it may have succeeded.
(*WE*)

As usual, Greene's appraisal of his work is extremely accurate: the novel's main strength is undoubtedly in the elegiac account of the ageing Castle's doomed love for his young wife Sarah. In *The*

Honorary Consul Greene had shown the possibility of happiness in love, but it was a blighted happiness. In *The Human Factor,* however, a picture of true happiness in the love between two individuals is drawn, and unlike earlier Greene heroes, such as Scobie and Charley Fortnum, Castle does not confuse pity with love ('It wasn't pity, any more than it had been pity when he fell in love with Sarah pregnant by another man'). He is, however, acutely aware of the link between love and fear, having learned in South Africa 'the age-old lesson that fear and love are indivisible'. Castle is afraid that the past will catch up with them and that his treachery, the payment he makes in return for that love being possible, will be discovered. As we have seen in the Introduction, success for Greene is intrinsically linked with failure; if his characters enjoy happiness then they must also be deprived of it, for that is the nature of life. Thus Castle had always felt 'that one day a doom would catch up on them', and the novel is about that moment of doom.

In *The Heart of the Matter* Greene portrayed a man who committed the worst of all sins in the eyes of the Church, the 'unforgivable sin' of despair, with such sympathy that it was impossible to accept the Church's ruling that he would be damned for eternity. Now in *The Human Factor* he is portraying a man who commits the most serious of all crimes in the eyes of the state, treason, and again allows the reader to see into 'what they call the heart of the matter', so that it is as impossible to condemn Castle for his actions as it was to condemn Scobie for his.

Like several other Greene heroes, Castle is reluctantly forced to become 'involved', to take sides, not for ideological but for personal reasons. In a review of Philby's own memoirs Greene asked, 'who among us has not committed treason to something or someone more important than a country?' In Greene's fiction the 'more important' private world of individuals is opposed to and threatened by the great hostile public world of politics and violence, and Castle's allegiance to the private world and betrayal of the public is a sign of his humanity, and recalls Wormold's declaration of individuality in *Our Man in Havana,* Greene's other spy novel: 'If I love or hate, let me love or hate as an individual. I will not be 59200/5 in anyone's global war.' The same point is made more subtly here by Sarah, when Castle tells her what he has done:

'Well, I'm what's generally called a traitor.'
'Who cares?' she said. She put her hand in his: it was an act more intimate than a kiss – one can kiss a stranger. She said, 'We have our own country. You and I and Sam. You've never betrayed that country, Maurice.'

Compared to the traitor, Castle, there are many reliable, trustworthy men in the Service who do not owe their allegiance to anything 'more important than a country'. These are the sad, lonely figures like Davis or Daintry, the Security Officer, neither of whom has any personal tie – the root of all treason according to Conrad, in a passage taken as the epigraph to the novel: 'I only know that he who forms a tie is lost. The germ of corruption has entered into his soul.'

The officer most immune to 'corruption' is Doctor Percival, who has no personal commitments whatsoever. In him Greene has created a vivid, frightening portrait of a ruthless institutional mind, a man who will serve his paymasters rightly or wrongly, a man with no regard for humanity. He justifies any action in the course of duty with cold logic, as when he explains his philosophy of 'little boxes' to Daintry, using the abstract painting by Ben Nicholson to demonstrate how no one need feel responsible for his actions. Percival is a man not only without ideals, but without morals or conscience, and is one of Greene's most successful portraits of 'Perfect evil walking the world, where perfect good can never walk again.'

In *The Human Factor* Greene's powers of characterization are at their highest. Many rounded characters emerge, and again Greene shows himself to be particularly adept at depicting unhappiness and misery: the sad figure of Daintry as the outsider at his daughter's wedding; Percival escaping the world through his fishing; Davis's hopeless pursuit of his secretary, Cynthia, and his dream of being sent to Lourenço Marques; Castle's widowed mother with her middle-class rigidity and intolerance of Sarah, and her final outrage at Castle's treachery.

In his earlier novels Greene tended to force characters to express his own moral point of view, with the result that they came close to caricatures. Here, however, although the moral vision is still as strong, he is writing as a realist rather than as a moralist; the characters are still actors but they speak with their own words rather than with Greene's; they breathe their own sighs of despair, not their author's.

The Human Factor continues the authorial game of referring back to earlier novels and to events in the author's own life that had begun in *Travels with My Aunt.* Most noticeably, it is set in Berkhamsted, where Greene had grown up and as a boy played at spies on the Common. There are other references, too, especially to *The End of the Affair,* the novel in which he first mapped out the world of domestic English middle-class romance, to which he returns here: characters have the same names – Sarah and Maurice – while one, Doctor Barker, has a flaming birth mark on his cheek like Smythe. Like Sarah too, Castle enters a church to ask for help but finds only 'a blank wall' (the priest tells him he needs a doctor and slams the shutter of the confessional in his face). Situations and phrases at several points contain faint echoes of previous fictions, and this has led some critics to accuse Greene of self-parody in his later books. That they are consciously and ironically self-referential; that they rework certain themes (such as treachery and betrayal) treated in earlier work, and use similar conventions and situations, there is no denying; but 'parody' implies an empty mimicry, and 'self-parody' a sense of having reached the end, and such a charge against novels with the subtlety, originality and depth of *The Comedians, The Honorary Consul* and *The Human Factor* is totally inadmissible.

III

After *The Human Factor* Greene, now in his seventy-third year, assumed that his career as a novelist was finished. However, on Christmas Day, 1978, a new book 'came without any warning' into his mind and almost exactly fifty years after the publication of his first novel he began to write his twenty-fourth.

Doctor Fischer of Geneva or The Bomb Party was unexpected in more than one way, however, for it is unlike anything Greene

had written before. Described by the author as a 'black entertainment', it is a simple, contrived fable, as unsettling as it is
amusing, about the nature of human love and hate, and about the
power of wealth to corrupt. It is a short book, a novella, in which
Greene's style is uncharacteristically bare. The setting is only
briefly sketched – Geneva, the bland, faceless centre of international capitalism – and we are told comparatively little about
the characters, their past, their private worlds, their thought
processes. Rather as in a play, the dialogue and stage directions
are given, but the only character we actually get 'inside' is Jones,
the narrator. He is a newcomer to Doctor Fischer's world and not
much interested in its inhabitants, but even his wife Anna-Luise,
who is Doctor Fischer's estranged daughter, remains an ill-
defined, shadowy figure.

Doctor Fischer is a self-made millionaire, thanks to his invention of Dentophil Bouquet, 'a toothpaste which was supposed to
hold at bay the infections caused by eating too many of our
chocolates', writes Jones, who works as a translator in a Swiss
chocolate factory. Dental decay is one of Greene's 'obsessions',
recurring regularly in his fiction as an image of human mortality
and, particularly in *The Power and the Glory,* of man's spiritual
corruption. Greene's purpose is surely symbolic, therefore, as
well as comic, in choosing to make his evil capitalist a toothpaste
manufacturer, a person who 'profits' from decay. Doctor Fischer
is, like Doctor Percival, another portrait of 'perfect evil'. He is a
man full of hatred and contempt, whose enormous wealth
enables him to indulge a taste for humiliating people by throwing
'parties', at which his 'toads' allow themselves to be humiliated in
return for the extravagant 'gifts' he presents to them. Fischer, in
his megalomania, likens himself to God, who also has an
inexhaustible 'greed' for 'our humiliation':

'The world grows more and more miserable while he twists the endless
screw, though he gives us presents – for a universal suicide would defeat
his purpose – to alleviate the humiliations we suffer.'

Fischer himself has suffered a great humiliation, the fact that
his wife Anna had found comfort and innocent companionship
with a poor clerk, Steiner, as an 'alleviation' of the loneliness and

suffering she had had to endure with him. In revenge for this he had Steiner sacked and made his wife even more miserable so that 'like an African' she willed herself to die. The 'disappoint-ment' of his wife's apparent betrayal led him to despise not just her and Steiner, but everyone:

'When one despises, Jones, it's like a deep and incurable wound, the beginning of death. And one must revenge one's wound while there's still time. When the one who inflicted it is dead, one has to strike back at others. Perhaps, if I believed in God, I would want to take my revenge on him for having made me capable of disappointment . . .'

In *The Human Factor* Greene showed a happy married-love affair which carried the seeds of its own destruction. In *Doctor Fischer of Geneva* Jones and Anna-Luise enjoy a similar happi-ness, a 'present' from God which also is inevitably destroyed, this time by Anna-Luise's death in a meaningless accident on the ski slope. Jones sees this as an act of cosmic injustice against which it is impossible to protest. The only revenge one can take is in a bitterness like Doctor Fischer's and in the same humiliation of others through the power of money. Thus, in a moment of bitterness, Jones humiliates the waiter by throwing the fifty-centime piece on the floor for him to pick up. He is ashamed of the action but also recognizes that if he were as rich as Fischer, with the same capacity for dominating the lives of others, he would have been tempted to share Fischer's form of revenge:

But if it had been in my power I would have revenged myself for what had happened on all the world – like Doctor Fischer, I thought, just like Doctor Fischer.

The nature of Fischer's contempt for humanity is thus under-stood by Jones and the picture of Fischer as totally evil is correspondingly diminished. Also, Fischer's jealousy of Steiner, like Plarr's jealousy of Fortnum in *The Honorary Consul,* shows that he is at least capable of love, as do his tears at his wife's funeral (though these are left in doubt – he may have had hay-fever). His final contempt for himself and his 'courageous' suicide show too that he is not entirely without a moral conscience.

For Steiner, the clerk, Fischer is like 'God Almighty' and he decides to take revenge on him for the misery and injustice he has caused, by spitting in his face: this is the pitiful, pointless revenge of the impotent against the omnipotent. However, when it comes to the act Steiner cannot do it, for Fischer has come full circle and now despises even himself, with the result that Steiner only pities him. The reader is reminded of Father Rivas in *The Honorary Consul* who believes in 'the evil of God' and pities Him. But there is nothing divine about Fischer, despite his pretensions to imitating God and despite Jones's portrayal of him both directly and indirectly as an all-powerful 'God-Almighty', controlling men through his wealth, and as a parody of Christ presiding over the Last Supper:

He raised the Christmas cracker rather as the priest at midnight Mass had raised the Host, as though he intended to make a statement of grave importance to a disciple – 'This is my body.'

However, when at the end Fischer shoots himself, the mortality of human evil is affirmed:

I looked at the body and it had no more significance than a dead dog. This, I thought, was the bit of rubbish I had once compared in my mind with Jehovah and Satan.

Although not a God, Fischer, as a multi-millionaire, is at least one of the High Priests of Mammon, the false God of 'the toads', the rich people who attend his parties and who willingly suffer the humiliations he inflicts on them in return for his God-like 'gifts'. In the toads we have an image of despair: human beings consumed by their own greed, for which they willingly sacrifice their dignity and are even prepared to risk their lives. In them is shown the absolute power of money to corrupt. Fischer, who thinks that every man has his price, concludes that his great mistake was in ruining Steiner, in giving him the dignity of poverty, rather than corrupting him and his love with riches and thus bringing him under his control:

'I should have told Kips to double your salary and I could have presented Anna with all the Mozart records she wanted. I could have bought you and her, like I bought all the others . . .'

The only person Fischer realizes he cannot buy is Jones ('It's too late now to buy you') because, with the death of Anna-Luise, Jones has lost the will to live. However, even earlier in the story, especially at the porridge party, Jones shows himself to be untempted by all Fischer's offers of riches, for he values his love for Anna-Luise more and knows that the acceptance of her father's offers would destroy it. As in Greene's other books, man's capacity to save himself is equal to his capacity to love: Jones's resistance to corruption corresponds to the strength of his love for Anna-Luise.

With the death of Doctor Fischer, Jones's hatred of him also dies, but his love for Anna-Luise lives on as memory. There are strong religious overtones in Jones's account of this memory: photographs of Anna-Luise, as well as her kitchen and her chair, are compared to religious relics, and he finds himself repeating a line from the Mass: 'As often as you do these things, you shall do them in memory of me.' The final vision of Jones is, however, as despairing as that of Maurice Castle. Both are old men, lonely, abandoned and without faith, waiting for death which, in Jones's case, was 'no longer an answer – it was an irrelevance':

Courage is sapped by day-to-day mind-dulling routine, and despair deepens so much every day one lives, that death seems in the end to lose its point. I had felt Anna-Luise close to me when I held the whisky in my hand and again when I pulled the cracker with my teeth [his two attempts at suicide], but now I had lost all hope of ever seeing her in any future. Only if I had believed in a God could I have dreamt that the two of us would ever have that *jour le plus long*. It was as though my small half-belief had somehow shrivelled with the sight of Doctor Fischer's body. Evil was as dead as a dog and why should goodness have more immortality than evil?

Jones is without belief, without God in the world and therefore without hope; deprived of his existential 'alleviation' in the form of the woman he loves, he must face alone a life of emptiness and deepening despair.

IV

As in *Doctor Fischer,* Greene's style in *Monsignor Quixote* is uncharacteristically spare, with a plot of extreme simplicity and an even greater reliance on dialogue. Father Quixote, the innocent, elderly parish priest of El Toboso (Don Quixote's village in the plains of La Mancha) is unexpectedly and farcically promoted to the rank of Monsignor by an even more unworldly visiting bishop from Rome, whose car Father Quixote 'fixes' (that is to say, fills with petrol). The promotion enrages Father Quixote's own bishop, who already considers the country priest to be simple-minded and unreliable, largely because of his claim that he is descended from the great Don Quixote himself ('How can he be descended from a fictional character?' asks the exasperated bishop), but also because of his friendship with the Communist ex-mayor of El Toboso. By extraordinary coincidence (and the book is full of these) the Mayor's name is Zancas, Sancho Panza's surname in Cervantes's 'truthful history', and so the priest of course calls him Sancho. He also calls his ageing Seat 600 Rocinante, after Don Quixote's own trusty mount.

Having been suspended from duty by the bishop, Monsignor Quixote and Sancho set off in Rocinante on a journey to Madrid and Salamanca. This is a journey through the Spain of the immediate post-Franco years, the late 1970s, and Greene paints a vivid portrait of a country in transition, though still a country of stark contrasts and divisions. Evidences of the political and social hangover of Francoism remain. The Civil Guards are deeply suspicious of a Monsignor consorting with a known Communist. They continually harass the pair and finally chase them after the Monsignor has disrupted a village fiesta in which the local priests demean the image of the Virgin by auctioning her to the highest bidder. The Monsignor and the mayor evade the pursuing *Guardia* by beating them into the grounds of the Trappist monastery at Osera in Galicia, where they claim sanctuary. However, the chase ends in a crash which neither Rocinante nor the Monsignor survive, for after celebrating a bizarre Mass with an imaginary eucharist while in a state of delirium, the priest dies.

On their travels Monsignor Quixote and Sancho visit the Vallée de los Caídos, the ostentatious mausoleum/monument in which Franco lies buried, and also the small simple grave of Miguel de Unamuno, the brilliant Catholic philosopher who was one of tyranny's most vociferous opponents during the Spanish Civil War. The conversation on the journey between Monsignor Quixote and Sancho, and indeed the whole novel, is dominated by the shadows of these two historical figures.

This conversation between Catholic and Communist is central to the thematic structure of the novel as it explores the relationship between religious belief and political commitment, continuing the debate between politics and religion which has been a feature of Greene's work since the 1930s. Sancho, the Communist, argues for a political, historical remedy to the problems of human society. He is a rational humanist who sees the root cause of the problem in social injustice – and the solution in the practical application of Marxist theory. Monsignor Quixote, on the other hand, has no confidence in anything but the power of faith and prayer, and in the reward of eternal life beyond this world.

Both the mayor and the priest, however, are no longer secure in their respective beliefs and during the course of their journey together their growing doubts serve to draw them together. Soon after they have set off on their travels, Monsignor Quixote dreams of 'a deepening friendship and a profounder understanding, of a reconciliation even between their disparate faiths'. Their friendship does grow and this leads in turn to a greater willingness to understand and respect each other's beliefs.

The priest is a political innocent, though his innocence is not of the 'dangerous' kind portrayed in *The Quiet American,* but a genuine, childlike simplicity and goodness of soul. When he leaves the cloistered life as parish priest of El Toboso and travels, he passes from the world of innocence to that of experience. As he does so he decides that 'one cannot be neutral', like Pilate, 'when it comes to choosing between good and evil', and he begins to understand better the need for political action, which he himself takes against the villagers who dress the statue of the Virgin Mary in banknotes at the village fiesta. At this moment, driving towards the fiesta, intent, like his noble ancestor, on rescuing a maiden's honour, he says to the mayor: 'There are moments . . . when I am inclined to address you as *compañero* ['comrade'], but not yet, not yet.'

Although in no way 'converted' to the mayor's 'faith', Monsignor Quixote reaches a greater understanding of Marx, and he finds his writings 'Quixotic' in the same way as the mayor compares the priest's books of theology to Don Quixote's books on the code of chivalry, which even in Cervantes's day was hopelessly outdated and irrelevant. As Monsignor Quixote approaches death and in his delirium celebrates Mass, he shows that his dream of understanding and reconciling the two faiths has been achieved. He 'consecrates' an imaginary host and presents it to the Communist, whom he addresses finally as 'comrade', and who accepts it out of personal love for the priest: ' "*Compañero* . . . you must kneel, *compañero.*" He came forward three steps with two fingers extended, and the Mayor knelt. Anything which will give him peace, he thought . . .'

The unbelieving mayor claims that even if 'Descartes is right' and he has indeed received the eucharist (even though it did not physically exist) it has no significance for him. There is an echo here from *The End of the Affair,* however, as the reader recalls the 'magical' effect of another sacrament, baptism, in the face of disbelief in that novel. The mayor's motive for accepting the host from Monsignor Quixote was love for his friend, and through this love he is brought back to God despite himself. This is made clear by the nature of 'Sancho's reward' – which is also the final destination of their travels, the Kingdom of God:

'I don't offer you a governorship, Sancho. I offer you a kingdom.'
'Speak to him,' Father Leopoldo urged.
'A kingdom?' Sancho repeated.
'Come with me, and you will find the kingdom.'
'I will never leave you, father . . .'

Although clearly inspired by Cervantes's *Don Quixote,* Greene's novel is thematically influenced more by another great Spanish writer, Unamuno, and, in particular, by two of his works: *The Tragic Sense of Life* and *Our Lord Don Quixote* (and Greene underlines this influence by making Unamuno the mayor's one-time professor at the University of Salamanca – of which Unamuno was in fact Rector – and by various other allusions to him as 'one of our great modern philosophers', and so on). The main theme of *Monsignor Quixote* is the nature of belief and the modern believer's inevitable struggle in a rational world against uncertainty and disbelief – whether that belief is in 'the God who died' or 'the God who failed'. Both Monsignor Quixote and the mayor find their faiths to be based on uncertainty, which with despair is, according to Unamuno, the driving force of true faith. At first worried by his uncertainties, which begin as he drives away from El Toboso, Monsignor Quixote soon begins to realize that 'it is human to doubt': 'Oh, I want to believe that it is all true – and that want is the only certain thing I feel.' There is in this a clear echo of Unamuno:

. . . Faith is in essence no more than a matter of will, not one of reason, just as to believe is to want to believe, and that to believe in God is to wish, above all and before all, that there may be a God.

Father Quixote progresses to an even more Unamunian position after his dream of total certainty which was like 'a kind of Saharan desert without doubt or faith'. It has now become for him 'an awful thing not to have doubts' and he prays, 'God save me from such a belief'. As they stand over Unamuno's grave at Salamanca, Monsignor Quixote attacks the mayor for his 'complete belief' which is devoid of uncertainty and therefore lacking 'the dignity of despair'. In reply the mayor confesses his own uncertainties and quotes the words of his old professor (from *The Tragic Sense of Life*) – which greatly impress the priest:

'Have I complete belief?' Sancho asked. 'Sometimes I wonder. The ghost of my professor haunts me. I dream I am sitting in his lecture room and he is reading to us from one of his own books. I hear him saying, "There is a muffled voice, a voice of uncertainty which whispers in the ears of the believer. Who knows? Without this uncertainty how could we live?" '

Unamuno's inspired and witty exegesis of *Don Quixote* has clearly influenced too Greene's reading of that work, and Unamuno here might be describing not Don Quixote and Sancho Panza, but Monsignor Quixote, 'touched by the wing-tip . . . of despair', and the rationalist ex-mayor of El Toboso:

Our Lord Don Quixote is the prototype of the vitalist whose faith is founded on uncertainty, and Sancho is the prototype of the rationalist who doubts his own reason.

As they each acknowledge their own doubts, both Monsignor Quixote and the mayor become aware of how their uncertainties can serve to bring them together:

It's odd, he thought, as he steered Rocinante with undue caution round a curve, how sharing a sense of doubt can bring men together perhaps even more than sharing a faith. The believer will fight another believer over a shade of difference: the doubter fights only with himself.

It is hard to find certain belief among Greene's characters, and those who do possess it unmistakably have the disapproval of the author; for example, the pious women in *The Power and the Glory,* or Pyle in *The Quiet American.* In *Monsignor Quixote* certain belief is represented by the Bishop and Father Herrera, a zealous priest sent to replace Monsignor Quixote in El Toboso. They are members of the traditional Spanish Church which supported General Franco, as the Bishop is fond of recalling, and are mocked as representatives of the Church of rigid ideology – the same church that Greene depicted in his earlier Catholic novels (there is an ironic suggestion of this rigidity in Father Herrera's name, which derives from the Spanish *hierro,* 'iron'). It is this Church which, to quote Father Rank in *The Heart of the Matter,* 'knows all the rules' and which, with its unbending system of divine punishment and reward, makes God the judge and gaoler of his creatures, a system which is profoundly questioned in all of Greene's 'Catholic' writings. This rigidity is derided in *Monsignor Quixote* as Sancho picks out the hilarious absurdities from that 'sound' authority on moral theology, Father Heribert Jone, who is as unreasonable, and menacing, as the Civil Guards who harass the travellers for no good reason. These *Guardias* are the secular, political equivalent of the Bishop and Father Herrera as they work together to defeat Father Quixote's attempt to liberate himself, both physically and mentally, from the Church's dogmatism. Another passage from *The Tragic Sense of Life* has reverberations here:

. . . We are not concerned with some transcendental police system, nor
with considering God as Great Judge or Civil Guard, that is, we are not
concerned with heaven and hell as devices to shore up our paltry
mundane morality . . .

Although *Monsignor Quixote* is, more than anything, a debate
between the two beliefs, between rational humanism and Roman
Catholicism, and a dialogue on uncertainty and despair as the
basis of modern faith, the two debaters are, to use one of
Unamuno's favoured phrases, men of flesh and blood, and are
two of Greene's most rounded, and likeable, creations. The
background setting of Spain, still suffering the hangover of Fascism
after the death of Franco in 1975, is also vividly evoked and just
as the author seems to have a great affection for the characters of
Father Quixote and Sancho, he also displays an affection for
their country:

'How little Spain changes,' the Mayor said. 'You would never feel in
France that you were in the world of Racine or Molière, nor in London
that you were still close to Shakespeare's time. It is only in Spain and
Russia that time stands still.'

Although superficially highly realistic, *Monsignor Quixote*
undermines traditional realism in several ways. There are the
ironical self-references we have come to expect in Greene's later
work, which some have called self-parody ('In your company I
fear if I'm not careful I shall become what I've heard called a
whisky priest'). But more important is the way in which fact and
fiction are confused in the novel.

For Unamuno Don Quixote was as 'real as Cervantes', just as
his own fictional characters were as real as himself, and this
reality of fictional characters has been a recurring theme in
Greene's novels since Wormold's fantasies came alive in *Our
Man in Havana* and since Henry Pulling, in *Travels with My
Aunt,* realized that 'Hamlet is no less real now than Winston
Churchill, and Jo Pulling no less historical than Don Quixote.' In
Monsignor Quixote a 'real person' claims to be descended from a
fictional character and this, quite naturally, is seen as fantastic
and even 'mad' – until the reader pauses to reconsider and
remembers that of course the priest too is a fictional character

and therefore is indisputably a descendant of the great Don. Reality is further confused by the appearance in this fictional world of genuine historical figures: Unamuno is Sancho's teacher at the university.

In such a world it is impossible to be certain what is real and what is imaginary, what is natural and what is supernatural. Did Monsignor Quixote really turn a non-existent host into the body of Christ in his imaginary Mass, asks the Trappist 'student of Descartes', Father Leopoldo?

'Do you think it's more difficult to turn empty air into wine than wine into blood? Can our limited senses decide a thing like that? We are faced by an infinite mystery.'

For Father Leopoldo 'fact and fiction' are indistinguishable. In the end, he says, 'you have just to choose.' It is this uncertainty of reality and therefore of absolute truth which has led him to 'leap' into faith. Like many of Greene's Catholic characters, Father Leopoldo chooses the mystery for what it is, accepting the inability of man to define or describe it. He has 'jumped' into faith, just as Sarah in *The End of the Affair* 'fell' into it, regardless of the theologians whose arguments are based on the separateness of reality and unreality.

In *A Sort of Life* Greene wrote about the difference between a writer's first novel, which is 'an adventure', and his later work which is a duty:

The first is like a sprint which leaves you exhausted and triumphant beside the track. With the second the writer has been transformed into a long-distance runner – the finishing tape is out of sight, at the end of life.

Although there is no reason to believe that *Monsignor Quixote* is Greene's 'finishing tape' (on the contrary, in an interview in June 1986 he declared that he was in fact working on another novel) it is undeniably a triumphant last sprint which displays no sign of exhaustion, for it is one of Greene's best and most amusing novels and one in which the disparate elements of his personal commitment to life are expressed with characteristic force.

Bibliography

Works by Graham Greene

Novels

The Man Within (Heinemann, London, and Doubleday, New York, 1929)

The Name of Action (Heinemann, London, 1930; Doubleday, New York, 1931)

Rumour at Nightfall (Heinemann, London,1931; Doubleday, New York, 1932)

Stamboul Train (Heinemann, London, 1932; published as *Orient Express*, Doubleday, New York, 1933)

It's a Battlefield (Heinemann, London, and Doubleday, New York, 1934)

England Made Me (Heinemann, London, and Doubleday, New York, 1935)

A Gun for Sale (Heinemann, London, 1936; as *This Gun for Hire*, Doubleday, New York, 1936)

Brighton Rock (Heinemann, London, and Viking Press, New York, 1938)

The Confidential Agent (Heinemann, London, and Viking Press, New York, 1939)

The Power and the Glory (Heinemann, London, 1940; as *The Labyrinthine Ways,* Viking Press, New York, 1940)

The Ministry of Fear (Heinemann, London, and Viking Press, New York, 1943)

The Heart of the Matter (Heinemann, London, and Viking Press, New York, 1948)

The Third Man (Viking Press, New York, 1950)

The Third Man and *The Fallen Idol* (Heinemann, London, 1950)

The End of the Affair (Heinemann, London, and Viking Press, New York, 1951)

The Quiet American (Heinemann, London, 1955; Viking Press, New York, 1956)

Loser Takes All (Heinemann, London, 1955; Viking Press, New York, 1957)

Our Man in Havana (Heinemann, London, and Viking Press, New York, 1958)

A Burnt-Out Case (Heinemann, London, and Viking Press, New York, 1961)

The Comedians (The Bodley Head, London, and Viking Press, New York, 1966)

Travels with My Aunt (The Bodley Head, London, 1969; Viking Press, New York, 1970)

The Honorary Consul (The Bodley Head, London, and Simon and Schuster, New York, 1973)

The Human Factor (The Bodley Head, London, and Simon and Schuster, New York, 1978)

Doctor Fischer of Geneva or the Bomb Party (The Bodley Head, London, and Simon and Schuster, New York, 1980)

Monsignor Quixote (The Bodley Head, London, and Simon and Schuster, New York, 1982)

The Tenth Man (The Bodley Head and Anthony Blond, London, and Simon and Schuster, New York, 1985; written in 1944)

SHORT STORIES

Nineteen Stories (Heinemann, London, 1947; Viking Press, New York, 1949)

Twenty-One Stories (Heinemann, London, 1954; Viking Press, New York, 1962)

A Sense of Reality (The Bodley Head, London, and Viking Press, New York, 1963)

May We Borrow Your Husband? (The Bodley Head, London, and Viking Press, New York, 1967)

Collected Stories (The Bodley Head, London, 1972; Viking Press, New York, 1973)

PLAYS

The Great Jowett (Play for radio broadcast by the BBC, 1939)
The Living Room (Heinemann, London, 1953; Viking Press, New York,
    1954)
The Potting Shed (Viking Press, New York, 1957; Heinemann, London,
    1958)
The Complaisant Lover (Heinemann, London, 1959; Viking Press, New
    York, 1961)
Carving a Statue (The Bodley Head, London, 1964)
The Return of A. J. Raffles (The Bodley Head, London, 1975; Simon
    and Schuster, New York, 1976)
Yes and No (The Bodley Head, London, 1983)
For Whom the Bell Chimes (The Bodley Head, London, 1983)

AUTOBIOGRAPHY

A Sort of Life (The Bodley Head, London, and Simon and Schuster,
    New York, 1971)
Ways of Escape (The Bodley Head, London, 1980; Simon and Schuster,
    New York, 1981)
L'autre et son double (Belfond, 1981, translated as *The Other Man:
    Conversations with Graham Greene* by Marie-Françoise Allain,
    The Bodley Head, London, and Simon and Schuster, New
    York, 1983)

TRAVEL

Journey Without Maps (Heinemann, London, and Doubleday, New
    York, 1936)
The Lawless Roads (Heinemann, London, 1939; as *Another Mexico*,
    Viking Press, New York, 1939)
In Search of a Character: Two African Journals (The Bodley Head,
    London, 1961; Viking Press, New York, 1962)

Babbling April (Basil Blackwell, Oxford, 1925). Poems.

British Dramatists (Collins, London, 1942; included in *The Romance of English Literature*, Hastings House, New York, 1944)

Why Do I Write? (Percival Marshall, London, and British Book Centre, New York, 1948)

The Lost Childhood (Eyre & Spottiswoode, London, 1951; Viking Press, New York, 1952). Essays.

Collected Essays (The Bodley Head, London, and Viking Press, New York, 1969)

The Pleasure Dome: Collected Film Criticism, 1935–1940, edited by John Russell-Taylor (Secker & Warburg, London, 1972; as *Graham Greene on Film*, Simon and Schuster, New York, 1972)

Lord Rochester's Monkey (The Bodley Head, London, and Viking Press, New York, 1974; written *c*. 1934). Biography.

J'Accuse – The Dark Side of Nice (The Bodley Head, London, 1982)

Getting to Know the General (The Bodley Head, London, and Simon and Schuster, New York, 1985). Account of Greene's friendship with General Torrijos, President of Panama.

SELECTED CRITICISM

Books about Graham Greene and books containing chapters and articles about him.

Allott, Kenneth, and Farris, Miriam, *The Art of Graham Greene* (Hamish Hamilton, London, 1951)

Atkins, John, *Graham Greene* (Calder & Boyars, London, 1957; rev. 1966)

Cassis, A. F., *Graham Greene: An Annotated Bibliography of Criticism* (Metuchen, New Jersey, 1981)

DeVitis, A., *Graham Greene* (Twayne, Boston, 1964; rev. 1986)

Evans, Robert O., (ed.) *Graham Greene: Some Critical Considerations* (University of Kentucky Press, Lexington, 1963)

Gransden, K. W., 'Graham Greene's Rhetoric' (in *Essays in Criticism*, 1981)

Hynes, Samuel (ed.) *Graham Greene: A Collection of Critical Essays* (Prentice Hall, New Jersey, 1973). Essays by, among others: W. H. Auden; Richard Hoggart; Frank Kermode; François Mauriac; George Orwell; and Evelyn Waugh.

Johnstone, Richard, *The Will to Believe: Novelists of the 1930s* (Oxford University Press, Oxford, 1982)

Kunkel, Francis, *The Labyrinthine Ways of Graham Greene* (Sheed & Ward, New York, 1959)

Lewis, R. W. B. *The Picaresque Saint* (Barnes and Noble, New York, 1959)

Lodge, David, *Graham Greene* (Columbia University Press, 1966)

Nott, Kathleen, *The Emperor's Clothes* (Heinemann, London, 1953)

O'Faolain, Sean, *The Vanishing Hero* (Eyre and Spottiswoode, London, 1956)

Sharrock, Roger, *Saints, Sinners and Comedians*, (Burns and Oates, London, 1984)

Smith, Grahame, *The Achievement of Graham Greene* (Harvester Press, Brighton, 1985)

Spurling, John, *Graham Greene* (Methuen, London, 1983)

Stratford, Philip, *Faith and Fiction: Creative Process in Greene and Mauriac* (University of Notre Dame Press, Indiana, 1964)

Wyndham, Francis, *Graham Greene* (Longmans Writers and their Work series, 1955; rev. 1968)

Index